IAIN OUGHTRED

A LIFE IN WOODEN BOATS

IAIN OUGHTRED

A LIFE IN WOODEN BOATS

NIC COMPTON

WoodenBoat
BOOKS
BROOKLIN, MAINE USA
www.woodenboatbooks.com

Published by WoodenBoat Books
Naskeag Road, Great Cove Drive, PO Box 78
Brooklin, Maine 04616
www.woodenboatbooks.com

First edition 2008

ISBN 10: 0-937822-99-X
ISBN 13: 978-0937822-99-9

A CIP catalogue record for this book is available from the British Library.

This book is produced using paper that is made from wood grown in managed, sustainable forests. It is natural, renewable and recyclable. The logging and manufacturing processes conform to the environmental regulations of the country of origin.

Designed and typeset in Sabon 10.5pt
by Ben Cracknell Studios | www.benstudios.co.uk

Printed and bound in China by C&C Offset Printing Co Ltd

Cover photographs:
Front, top, © Kathy Mansfield: *Scalloway*, a Caledonian Yawl built by Frank Schofield (at the helm). Front, bottom, © Iain Oughtred: *Mairead*, an Elf design (faering type) built by Iain, on the beach in Findhorn. Back, main, © Nic Compton: *Mairead* on Findhorn Bay with her designer/builder on the oars. Front flap, © Iain Oughtred: Iain carving the stem of the prototype Ness Yawl, *Jeanie Henderson*. Back flap, top, © Tess Zahn: Nic Compton. Back flap, bottom, © Iain Oughtred: the 13ft Acorn design *Hoolet*, built at a boatbuilding workshop and owned first by Iain then Kathy Mansfield, pictured with Iain on board. Spine, © Iain Oughtred: Iain rowing the prototype Acorn Skiff, which launched his career.

NIC COMPTON/SALTY DOG MEDIA

This book is dedicated to Zennor and Sam,
two fine young crew in the making.

CONTENTS

PREFACE

ONE WINTER IN THE EARLY 1980s I was sent to England by the American magazine *WoodenBoat*. The editors gave me a pocketful of travellers' checks and a chit for a hire car with unlimited mileage. They told me to research a couple of specific articles, and then poke around for a few weeks and see if the English might be having a wooden boat revival similar to the one that had been underway in America since the early 1970s.

I bounced all over the country – Poole, Portsmouth, the Isle of Wight, Exeter, Truro, the Scilly Isles, Bristol, Liverpool, Windermere, Redcar, Whitby, Lowestoft, Ipswich, Mersea, Henley, Chatham, and no end of tiny backwater towns between. Not much was happening. Fibreglass was king. It was a period of nautical despair.

There was, however, a pocket of activity in Maldon, and one day, while exploring the waterfront in that town, I met Fabian Bush, a young boatbuilder. Fabian was of a type not uncommon at that time in America but an anomaly in England; a university graduate with a predilection for working with his hands. Through him I met Iain Oughtred, another anomaly; an aspiring designer of wooden rowing and sailing skiffs, double-paddle canoes, and other small, non-powered craft in an era when mainstream designers were concentrating on larger fibreglass motorboats and sailboats, preferably for cruising. While the mainstream designers worked in offices with assistants and the latest drafting and calculating conveniences, Iain had no fixed working (or living) address. He worked wherever he was at the time.

At that time he and Fabian were living in semi-poverty on Osea Island in the Blackwater River and building two Acorn skiffs, the design that would make Iain's reputation. Of lapstrake construction, planked in plywood, it was a fine-lined rowing and sailing craft that was beautiful in its simplicity. Yes, it was derivative – it owed much to several American boat types of the late-19th and early-20th centuries – but it was a step beyond anything that had come before. For a long time I couldn't put my finger on what made that skiff so striking, but after getting to know Iain both in England and in America, where he spent a year in the late 1980s, I came to realize that it was art that made it so.

Iain Oughtred is an artist, pure and simple, and his designs reflect that sensibility. Look at the sheer of the Acorn; the stem of the Grey Seal; the coaming of the MacGregor and its relationship to the sheer and the foredeck; the rudder and tiller of the Arctic Tern. These are the products of a man with an eye for a functional curve, the very essence of boat design and construction. To be successful all boat designs must meet certain technical criteria to do with stability, weight distribution, buoyancy, structural strength, etc., but to be memorable they must have heart, soul – an emotional centre – and only an artist can give them that.

I have great admiration for Iain Oughtred as an artist and a small-craft designer. I also have admiration for his having stuck to his principles all these years, for having gone his own way and being successful at it, and for achieving distinction without ever resorting to self-promotion. A book about his life and work is well worth the read.

Peter H Spectre
Spruce Head
Maine, USA

ACKNOWLEDGMENTS

One of the greatest pleasures in writing this book was meeting and talking to the people who have been involved in Iain's life. All were unanimously supportive of the project and unstintingly helpful. I'd like to thank them all, in particular: Welmoed Bouhuys, for her special insight; David Maslow, for his honesty; Elizabeth van Ekert, for her moderation; Bob Ross, for digging deep; Peter Spectre, for being in the right place at the right time – and recording it; Maynard Bray, for his enthusiasm; Jon Wilson, for his vision; Scot Bell, for his constructive criticism; Fabian Bush, for his eloquence; Charles-Henri Le Moing, for promoting the good cause; Anna Kisby, for her sharp eyes. I'd also like to thank Jamie Clay, Nigel Irens, Pete Greenfield, Jack Chippendale and Donna Braye of the Mosman Library. Last but not least, thanks to Liz Piercy and Janet Murphy for their support and encouragement – and for tolerating my writer's foibles. Thanks too to Iain for his time and hospitality, not least the vegetable stew and long johns.

Nic Compton

introduction

UN BON COUP DE CRAYON

ONE OF THE MORE ENJOYABLE ASPECTS of working at *Classic Boat* magazine in the early 1990s was attending the Greenwich Wooden Boat Show. Set on the lawns of the National Maritime Museum and surrounded by the spectacular buildings of the former Naval College, it was a gentle affair, where likeminded people could meet, well away from the plastic fantastics that dominated the mainstream shows. One of my tasks was to help organize the annual Amateur Boatbuilding Competition, which at its peak culminated with a display of a dozen or so boats lined up in front of the *Classic Boat* stand. Someone had the bright idea of holding the prize-giving in the hold of the *Cutty Sark*, which was preserved nearby, and for several years the party became the hot ticket of the show.

A surprising number of entries in the competition were designed by a 'Scottish' designer by the name of Iain Oughtred, so at my first show I made a point of seeking him out among the exhibitors. Standing beside a hand-painted sign bearing his name, I found a tall, wiry man with a matt of curly dark brown hair and frizzy beard. I introduced myself, and immediately found myself being appraised by a pair of cautious yet inquisitive brown eyes. His whole manner was guarded and aloof, but as we spoke and he realized that I knew a little bit about boats and boatbuilding – or at least could tell the difference between teak and mahogany – he relaxed a little, and by the time I left I was rewarded with a rare smile.

The following year, I invited him to be one of the judges for the Amateur Boatbuilding Competition and felt a great sense of personal and professional satisfaction when he accepted. Apart from having complete respect for his opinion on such matters, I knew that just having him on board would improve the credibility of the magazine in the boatbuilding world. By then I was familiar with many of his designs, such as the Acorn Skiff, the Mouse pram and the Whilly Boat, all of which had been exhibited at the show in various guises – and had become an admirer of his work.

But it wasn't until 1994 that I became a true convert. That year, a particularly handsome version of Iain's Caledonia Yawl was entered in the Amateur Boatbuilding Competition. Crisply painted in blue and white, with plain wooden thwarts and a carved tiller, *Eela* looked as if she was ready to take off on an adventure; any adventure. And, sure enough, her owner planned

The former naval college (now Greenwich University) provides an impressive backdrop for the Greenwich Wooden Boat Show. (Photo: Nic Compton.)

to take her on a cruise to the Baltic, possibly single-handed. Another more 'showy' Oughtred design won the competition that year (a very finely built Ptarmigan), but *Eela* won the popular vote – and stole my heart.

That same year, Iain brought his first Ness Yawl to Greenwich. *Jeanie Henderson* was a 'refined' version of the Caledonia Yawl, taking the Scottish sixareen 'to its logical conclusion', as I would later read. With her low sweeping sheer and impudent long stems, she looked like a mad, daring mini-Viking boat. In fact, although I didn't know it then, she was a logical expression of Iain's love of traditional craft and his lifelong infatuation with racing, all rolled into one. Compared with the safe, slightly twee boats being produced by most other traditional boat designers, she was a breath of fresh air. More than that, to my increasingly critical eyes she was one of the most exciting boats I had ever seen. I was thrilled by the idea that you could combine traditional aesthetics with high performance, and was delighted when I later heard that Iain had not only won a race at the Portsoy Traditional Boat Festival, but had lapped the entire fleet. It felt like a vindication of everything I believed in.

A few months after this double-whammy, I got my chance to try out one of Iain's boats on the water when I test sailed a Caledonia Yawl built in Norfolk by former businessman turned boatbuilder Frank Schofield. To make his boat more authentic, Frank had gone back to the original sixareens and reinstated some of the details that Iain had removed for the sake of

simplicity. *Scalloway* was very much an Oughtred design, but with the flat oars, wooden kabes (instead of rowlocks) and tapered gunwales of the Shetland boats. With her traditional unstayed lug rig and high freeboard, she was a joy to sail, making the most of the October breeze as we glided past the seals on Blakeney Point. Had I had the money, I would almost certainly have sailed home with her there and then.

This was a good time for Iain. Despite having found his vocation late in life (he was in his early 40s when he started designing boats in earnest) he had consolidated his reputation as one of the foremost pioneers of clinker plywood construction for amateurs. Since his breakthrough Acorn design of 1982 he had built up an extensive range of designs that he sold through *WoodenBoat* (America's leading traditional boat magazine) and his own design catalogue. By the early 1990s, he had built up a worldwide following for his graceful designs, with their comprehensive, well thought-through plans targeted at the amateur builder. Indeed, he was widely acknowledged as being one of the key figures behind the long-awaited wooden boat revival in the UK. On the personal front, he had an idyllic (albeit rented) home near Edinburgh in his beloved Scotland, and had regular help with both his draughting and boatbuilding work from a delightful young woman called Mary.

The previous ten years had brought no shortage of praise for his work. The Acorn Skiff, his first epoxy plywood construction, was described as a 'sweet-lined, slippery little jewel' by Maynard Bray in *WoodenBoat*. 'Iain Oughtred is a young Englishman who is crazy about small boats,' wrote Maynard. 'But, more than that, he is a talented designer of small craft with a good eye for form. He blends the past with the present, fully understands how boats should be put together, and most importantly, has taken the time to put it all down on paper in great detail.'

That was followed a few years later by a ten-page article in France's authoritative *Chasse Marée* magazine, which described his style as 'postmodern' but touched with 'an artistic sensibility'. The article went on to explain: 'Iain Oughtred has a good drawing style, a strong sense of form, and there's no doubt that his creations are worthy of the aesthetics of his sources of inspiration. One can make out the original craft, but the profile is even purer, almost stylized, retaining the essential elegance but with something undeniably modern. Some will find them a little dainty for the choppy waters of our Channel coasts. But Iain likes light, finely-shaped boats, and has plenty of arguments to make in their defence.'

Having fallen in love with his two double-enders, I became a fan of his work and promoted his designs through the magazine whenever I could. I didn't get around to visiting him until a few years later, however, by which time he had moved to a new home in Findhorn, on the north-east coast of Scotland. Aged 60, he had just launched his latest creation: a 15ft faering exquisitely built from larch-faced plywood. I spent several days interviewing him, trying to discover what made him tick. What I found was a man who was both intensely shy and private, yet at the same time startlingly frank and open; a man who barricaded himself away from the world, and yet also longed for recognition and human contact. A man both self-assured and self-knowing, yet still capable of being emotionally reticent and even self-destructive. As he spoke, I found his words tended to invite more questions than they provided answers; each layer opening up to reveal several more layers of complication underneath, like a glass onion.

Little did either of us know then that his good times would soon come to an end. Within a few months, he would lose the whole infrastructure that he had worked so hard to achieve and be forced to move to the other side of the country. For a man who struggled at the best of times with the day-to-day practicalities of existence, it would be a long, hard road to rebuilding his life. Yet rebuild it he did. By the time I visited him again, nearly ten years later, he had branched out into several new areas of design, including an exciting modern take on a traditional American sharpie, and was midway through updating his whole design catalogue – a massive undertaking that had already consumed the better part of six years.

Now approaching his 70th birthday, Iain is as much in demand as ever and, thanks to the Internet, receives orders for his designs from sixty countries around the world – from Japan to Papua New Guinea via America, Russia and the Solomon Islands. Despite competition from any number of would-be boat designers armed with a CAD program and a faint notion of what makes a pretty line, his hand-drawn designs remain at the pinnacle of small boat design. So what makes Iain's designs special? What makes him stand out from the crowd of designers all competing to express the essence of traditional small craft?

Peter Spectre was the journalist who 'discovered' Iain and his colleague Fabian Bush while exploring the mud banks of Britain's East Coast in the mid-1980s, and for him Iain's designs have an intuitive perfection. 'Like Francis Herreshoff, Iain is an artist. I remember seeing one of Herreshoff's Rozinantes being built, and her lines were so perfect that each plank just fell into place. It's the same with Iain – except that he does it with plywood. He was a pioneer of that style, and his designs have a fluency that come from a lifelong experience of sailing at all levels.'

Pete Greenfield, founder of *Classic Boat* and now editor of *Water Craft* magazine, ranks Iain in the top six small boat designers in the world. 'His boats are the height of the amateur boatbuilder's aspirations. They might start with another design because it's easier to build but, if they're successful, their ultimate goal is an Oughtred boat. They'll first build one in plywood then, if they manage that, their next goal will be to build one traditionally [ie using solid timber]. It's the ultimate test of their skills as an amateur boatbuilder.'

And it's not just the wooden boat aficionados who respond to his work. No less an authority than multihull designer Nigel Irens, who shared his flat with Iain in the early 1980s and went on to draw a string of famous yachts including Ellen MacArthur's record-breaking trimaran *B&Q*, is a fan. Describing Iain's 'holistic approach' to his work, he makes the point that not only are the designs attractive, but the drawings themselves are a pleasure to look at. 'It's very much boat as art, and it's all mixed in with the way he presents the drawings,' he says. 'He comes very much from the art spectrum of design, which is something I approve of.' Or, as *Chasse Marée* put it, Iain has 'un bon coup de crayon' (a nice touch with the pencil).

But, above all, Iain has integrity – by the bucketload. Integrity of vision, integrity of design, integrity of living, integrity of being. His view of life, essentially artisanal and 'green', runs through every aspect of the way he lives, from the food he eats to the books he reads, the music he listens to, the people he associates with, the boats he sails and, of course, the boats he draws. You may not agree with his point of view, but you can't accuse him of being disingenuous. It is this integrity, this sincerity, and the unique philosophy of life that it encompasses that make him such a fascinating subject. It's also what makes this book worth writing and, hopefully, will make it worth reading.

Nic Compton
Brighton

chapter 1
A CHILDHOOD NEAR THE SEA

SYDNEY IN THE 1950S was a great place for a boat-mad teenager to grow up. Sat within 188 miles of coastline, the city enjoyed the largest natural harbour in the world and the highest proportion of boat-owning citizens in the country. Elegant 1930s ferries plied the sparkling waters of Sydney Harbour, and many families had either a dinghy or small cruising boat to go and explore its multitude of creeks and inlets. For the serious sailor, there were dozens of racing classes to choose from, ranging from the famous skiffs, with their improbable clouds of canvas, to the more genteel 6-Metre class. Such was the explosion of interest in sailing in the area that the Yachting Association of New South Wales was created in 1953 and soon boasted over 100 member clubs.

For the young Iain Oughtred, sailing wasn't just a sport, it was his salvation. Born Ian Haig Outhred in Melbourne on 15 September 1939, he was the eldest of seven children – although his quiet nature was perhaps more befitting that of a younger member of the family. His father, Douglas Haig Outhred, worked as an accountant with an instrument-manufacturing firm, the

OPPOSITE Iain made his name first racing, then building, Gwen 12s on Sydney Harbour. (Photo: John Rose.)

BELOW On 21 June 1945, Douglas Haig Outhred is welcomed home from war by his sons Iain (left) and David. (Photo: courtesy Elizabeth Van Ekert.)

Thomas Optical and Scientific Company (TOSCO). Douglas was socially aspiring and liked to impress friends and family by having the right sort of furniture and the right sort of car. He was also a committed Christian, attending the local Presbyterian church, and became increasingly devout – if not fanatical.

Iain's mother Jean (née Henderson) was, by contrast, more unconventional and never quite fitted in with life in 1950s suburbia. Unlike Douglas, she was well educated and widely read, having majored in history at Melbourne University. She had a large collection of books, including a leather-bound complete works of Dickens, and longed to talk about such esoteric subjects as art, literature, religion, history and women's rights. Women weren't really expected to have an opinion on such subjects in Australian

male-dominated suburban society, however, and she was regarded as something of a renegade. To keep the peace, she kept her views to herself and went along with what Douglas wanted – including, it seemed, more and more children.

Two years after he was born, Iain was sent away to the country to stay with an aunt for two weeks. It was a place the family would return to often in the future and which they would grow to love, but Iain's first visit appears to have had a traumatic effect. When he returned to the family home, he found he was no longer the sole focus of his mother's attention; he had a new baby brother, David. The sensitive two-year-old took this apparent rejection to heart and became noticeably quieter and more introverted, a trait that was to remain with him well into adult life.

At this time, he developed another condition which was to haunt him for years to come: asthma. He had his first life-threatening attack soon after David was born and had recurring bouts throughout his time at school, to the point where his whole education was in jeopardy. The doctors put it down to allergies and subjected him to numerous tests to find the cause – although the real explanation, according to Iain, was staring them in the face. 'The doctors never noticed the wonderful coincidence that an asthma attack would always start on Monday morning, when I was supposed to go to school, and by about Friday, when school ended, it would be OK – always. They never noticed that!' he says. 'The more I thought about it, the more I reckoned it was almost entirely psychosomatic.'

By then, Douglas and Jean had four children (Iain, David, Rick and Elizabeth) and, despite the doctors advising Jean to stop there, three more were to follow (Margaret-Ann, Jennifer and Peter). From Iain's point of view, the growing family meant only one thing: less attention from his mother. As he puts it: 'I was her first baby, so when I was born she didn't know what to do and found it difficult to show affection because she had never even held a baby before. By the time she had seven children, she was too busy to show affection.'

Some good did come of Iain's asthma, however. As his attacks grew worse, the doctors recommended that he should live in warmer climes so, when TOSCO decided to open a branch in Sydney, Douglas jumped at the chance to run the new office. In 1949, the family moved north and found a house in Greenwich, on the lower North Shore of Sydney, where they lived for a couple of years, before moving to Wollstonecraft, slightly nearer the city centre, where they lived for the next 16 years.

The house at 39 Belmont Avenue (since torn down to make way for a block of flats) had been owned by a former Lord Mayor of Sydney and still had aspirations of grandeur. Built from a dark, purplish brick, with a huge terracotta tiled roof, the front of the building had intricate carved wood detailing and a small veranda. Inside, the parquet floor and bay windows gave the downstairs room an ostentatious elegance,

The Outhred family shortly before moving to Sydney in 1949. Left to right: David, Jean, Douglas, Rick and Iain. (Photo: courtesy Iain Oughtred.)

although the rest of the house was by contrast slightly shabby and unkempt. Iain and Rick slept upstairs in the loft rooms (along with a family of tarantulas), while the rest of the family slept on the first floor. A large basement contained several unfinished rooms which opened onto the back yard and, just beyond, the wild Australian bush. It was every bit the aspiring middle class suburban house Douglas would have wanted for his ever-expanding family.

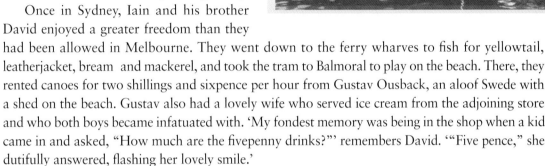

Once in Sydney, Iain and his brother David enjoyed a greater freedom than they had been allowed in Melbourne. They went down to the ferry wharves to fish for yellowtail, leatherjacket, bream and mackerel, and took the tram to Balmoral to play on the beach. There, they rented canoes for two shillings and sixpence per hour from Gustav Ousback, an aloof Swede with a shed on the beach. Gustav also had a lovely wife who served ice cream from the adjoining store and who both boys became infatuated with. 'My fondest memory was being in the shop when a kid came in and asked, "How much are the fivepenny drinks?"' remembers David. '"Five pence," she dutifully answered, flashing her lovely smile.'

There were also family holidays to the Blue Mountains and frequent trips to some of the many readily accessible beaches on the Sydney waterfront. It was the beginning of a deep relationship with the sea and nature which would have a profound effect not only on Iain but also, as he would learn much later, his mother.

ABOVE *Mosman was a popular boating area within easy access of Sydney city centre. (Photo: courtesy Mosman Local Studies Collection, Mosman Library.)*

LEFT *Balmoral Beach, on Sydney Harbour, where Iain and his brother David learned to sail. (Photo: courtesy Mosman Local Studies Collection, Mosman Library.)*

At the age of 12, however, Iain was sent to Sydney Grammar School, an independent college for boys based on the British public school model, which prized sporting prowess and academic achievement (in that order) above all else. Rugby and military cadet corp training was compulsory. For a creative child with poor social skills and no ability in sports such as rugby and athletics, it proved a painful ordeal. Until then, Iain had cruised through school relying on his natural intelligence and doing minimal work, but as the rigours of the grammar school system crushed down upon him, he grew increasingly disillusioned with studying and estranged from his peers.

'Every year, as it got more and more difficult, I slipped down one grade, starting in 2A, then 3B, and then 4C. To do well in exams, you had to do some work, but they were all subjects I had no interest in, so I didn't do any work. There were art and carpentry classes and a choir, but they were all after-school options, and I was anxious to get far away from the place as fast as I could!' he remembers. 'It was a strange situation. I was pretty much in an autistic state. Whether I would have been defined as such I don't know, but I was very isolated, doing my own thing, not saying anything to anyone, thinking my own thoughts and wondering why nobody else thought like I did.'

His single positive experience seems to have been reading a book of essays by Chesterton (who he describes as 'very intelligent, very perceptive and very humorous') whose liberal Christian views chimed with his own.

Iain scraped through his O Levels, with marks of around 53–57% – except for Latin, in which he got a memorable 2%, presumably for spelling his name right (he now reckons he should have got 'at least 4%'). Like millions of non-academic, non-sporting children before him and millions after, he would remember his school years as a complete waste of time. Worse still, the experience risked turning him into a social outcast. David sums up his brother's plight in no uncertain terms: 'Weakened by asthma, disinterested in team sports, and finding no academic, cultural, philosophical or religious influences that spoke to his inner truth, Iain had a lonely, insular childhood.'

His one major escape from academic meltdown, apart from his seaside rambles with his brother, was making model aeroplanes. His father Douglas had trained as an Air Force officer during the war, flying Mosquito fighter-bombers with the RAAF, and had passed on some of the romance of flying to his son. Iain started off by building balsa models of World War II aircraft from kits, and gradually, as his skills improved, moved on to gliders and small engine-powered planes. A friend of the family had worked in aircraft recognition during the war and had a book showing the silhouettes of all the military aircraft flying at the time. Iain borrowed the book and traced off the outlines of the planes and built his own scale models, a process which taught him basic design and construction skills which would become essential later in life. He proved adept at the task, and his brother remembers all his models being 'exquisitely' built. Meanwhile, at school, he joined the Air Training Corps and got a glimpse of the actual thing – enough to put him off joining the Royal Australian Air Force for real.

Model-making might have provided the lifeline Iain so badly needed, had it not been for his father's strong religious sensibilities. More passionate about his beliefs than ever, Douglas insisted that the whole family go to church on the Sabbath and that his children attend Sunday school. While Iain would have liked nothing better than to join the local model aeroplane flying club, the group met on a Sunday, and there was no way his father would allow him to take part in such a frivolous activity on such an important day. 'Observance of the

Sabbath,' wrote David, 'meant no beach, no rock 'n' roll, no model aircraft flying club, and no other such satanic ritual.'

Iain remembers his final 'flight' well. 'It was a Cessna Bird Dog, the nicest flying model I'd ever built. I decided to give it a test flight and put a tiny bit of fuel in the tank so it wouldn't go too far. I set the rudder one or two degrees to one side so that it would go up in a big circle and, when the fuel ran out, it would come back down in a spiral. I spent ages flicking and flicking it, trying to get the wretched engine going, and used up all the fuel. So I filled up the tank, gave it one flick, and away it went. Then I realized it had a full tank of fuel! It went up and up and up, and when it had used up all the fuel, went into a dead straight glide. It flew for miles and miles and miles, and was never seen again!'

There was another means of escape, however, and, living in Sydney, it was inevitable that Iain would eventually gravitate towards sailing. Sure enough, in his last year at school, he and David bought their first boat: a dilapidated Vaucluse Junior, better known as the 'VJ' class, called *Whisky*. The purchase price of £35 was advanced by their father and paid back from money earned on a paper round. The VJ was a 12ft Vee-bottomed dinghy designed by Charles Sparrow for the Vaucluse Amateur Sailing Club and was capable of up to 12 knots on the plane. No less an authority than America's Cup helmsman John Bertrand described the boat as: 'a speed

Iain (third from left) and his siblings on Balmoral Beach with his second boat: the 9ft Piccolo. (Photo: Douglas Oughtred.)

ABOVE *Skippers and friends of the Gwen fleet. (Photo: courtesy Elizabeth Van Ekert.)*

OPPOSITE, TOP *Iain on board his first Gwen 12, called* Fantasy, *which he fitted out himself. (Photo: Douglas Oughtred.)*

OPPOSITE, BOTTOM *Iain's lifelong fascination with motorbikes started aged 18, with a Lambretta. (Photo: Douglas Oughtred.)*

machine that can travel as fast as a Flying Dutchman. This is a high performance training boat, and its power to weight ratio is nothing short of phenomenal. One way or another they are hair-raising boats, and you need the nerve of a fighter pilot to sail them.'

It was an ambitious choice for a pair of complete beginners, as Iain soon found out. 'It was like a sailing surfboard; there was practically nowhere to sit, just a small hole on deck to put your feet in, and the crew had a sliding seat. There was a big ¼in steel centreplate, which made the boat desperately heavy and difficult to launch. On a lee shore in a fresh breeze, it would be leaping all over the place, while we were trying to manoeuvre the board into this tiny slot. The boat was very solid and very leaky – but heaps of fun.'

Despite having clearly bitten off more than they could chew, the brothers sailed the boat for a year or so, storing her on a rack for five shillings a week at Gustav Ousback's shed on Balmoral Beach, before Iain eventually bought another boat. Similar to the *Yachting World* Cadet but with a stem bow, *Piccolo* was much more manageable than the VJ and allowed him to join the junior racing programme at the prestigious Middle Harbour 16 Foot Skiff Sailing Club. It was here that he was introduced to racing for the first time and began to hone his sailing skills. He borrowed a rather sporty junior skiff from another club member and experienced the thrill of planing for the first time, which gave him a taste for high-performance sailing.

But, apart from the thrill of being on the water and the undoubted satisfaction of finding something else apart from model-making that he was good at, sailing represented something even more important to the lanky, self-conscious teenager: it was his bridge to the world. At last he had found fellow human beings who thought the way he thought (more or less) and who spoke the same language as he did (more or less). 'I never had the ability to communicate with people until I started sailing and talking to the guys at the sailing club,' he remembers. 'That was the first time I had conversations with other humans about anything that mattered to me.'

Again, his brother David puts it succinctly: 'Iain had little in common with his father, his friends, family, classmates, school curriculum, religion or society at large. In this context, he found one path that gave him a pastime, a passion, an identity, a craft, a social context. Model-making, then sailing, gave him a life.'

Iain had by then left school and, at the age of 15, got his first job – as a model-maker. It was an ideal first job, putting to use his self-taught skills building model aircraft and making the most of his eye for detail. The work ranged from representing architectural designs in 3D through to restoring the occasional model ship. His first big project was a set of five dioramas for the Petroleum Information Bureau, which depicted the different stages of oil manufacture, from the prehistoric age (complete with moving dinosaurs) to a desert scene, with pumps moving up and down, trucks driving back and forth and a DC3 flying overhead.

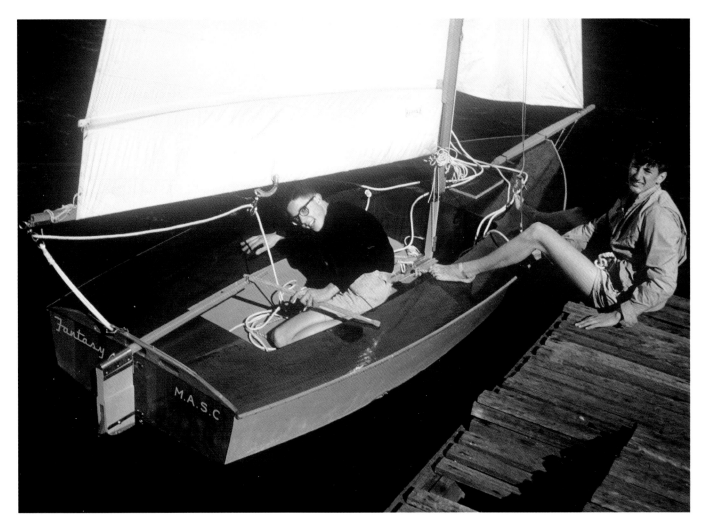

By now he had been well and truly bitten by the boating bug and even his father couldn't stop him sailing on a Sunday. The two of them eventually agreed on a compromise: Iain would pack all his sailing gear and take it with him to church. He would sit through the service and, as soon as it was over, he would rush down to the wharf and catch a ferry to the sailing club, changing into his sailing kit on the way.

His father may not have approved of him having fun on the Sabbath but, as teenage rebellions went, even he had to admit it was relatively harmless. They were formative times for the young Iain which taught him vital lessons in boat racing, design and general seamanship, as well as turning him from a lanky youth into a fit (though never really muscular) young man.

'There were no sailing schools in those days, no training boat classes, no lifejackets, no buoyancy – just an ancient

rescue boat. It meant you had to be more independent and gave a better education in sailing – provided you survived! There was generally a higher level of seamanship, and you learned things like never to leave your boat unless you have to – something many sailors had forgotten by the time it came to the disastrous Fastnet of 1979.

'I got to crew on one of the 16ft skiffs a few times, but I could never figure out how the helmsman signalled going about – it might have been a twitch of his eyebrow or a quiet grunt. I was the bailer boy, and kept being left on the wrong side because I couldn't work out when we were going about. Once, I was on the trapeze when the boat disappeared from under me – I looked down and there was just water. It turned out the centreboard case had collapsed. There was no buoyancy, so the boat was swamped and there was practically nothing above water. We were given a tot of rum and towed ashore.'

Piccolo soon gave way to a Mk II Moth called *Wasp*, a one-person racing dinghy that he kept at the Balmoral Sailing Club. Racing was forbidden to him, however, because it was on a Sunday and he couldn't violate his father's strict code. It did however spawn a lifelong fascination with the class. The solution eventually came when he joined the Mosman Amateur Sailing Club on Middle Harbour, which held its races on a Saturday. The club had just adopted the Gwen 12, a boxy but very lively 12ft dinghy which was beginning to dominate racing in both Melbourne and Sydney. Capable of over 20 knots, for a time it became known as the fastest 12-footer in the world. Iain bought a brand new hull from designer Charles Cunningham, which he fitted out himself and named *Fantasy*. With his brother installed as crew, he proceeded to do rather well in the local racing.

From sailing boats and building models, it was a short step to fulfilling his ultimate ambition: building a boat. His first project was a Sabot dinghy, built under his parents' house on Belmont Avenue. A smaller and more shapely version of the ubiquitous Mirror, the Sabot was a hard-chine 8ft pram widely used in Australia for sail training for children up to 16 years old. It was a modest venture, but Iain's craftsmanship was immediately apparent and the new owner promptly asked him to build a *Yachting World* keelboat. The improvised workshop under his parents' house was too small for such an ambitious undertaking, and besides, Iain didn't think he was up to the task yet, but other orders soon followed. A rival skipper at the Mosman Sailing Club was so impressed by the Sabot that he asked Iain to build him a new Gwen 12 – quite a show of faith in the novice boatbuilder and a commission Iain took on with delight, if a little trepidation. Again, the workshop proved a tad small for building a 12-footer, but he remedied the situation by knocking down part of a wall while his parents were on holiday.

After the success of his first two commissions, Iain decided to build a Gwen 12 for himself. Having raced the boats for three years, he knew what made them tick, and he was determined to build the fastest Gwen 12 possible for the national championships, due to take place in Sydney in the summer of 1960–1. He spent days working on the mast alone, shaving it down to make it more flexible, until it broke, and he had to build another one, just a little bit thicker. He went through three masts before finding the optimum dimension. His sailmaker, Gary Fogg, was impressed by his dedication and worked with him to achieve the ideal sail shape for the mast and the weight of the crew. By the time *Clementine* entered the championship she was a flyer, and Iain came from behind to win the final race, and the event, in spectacular fashion.

It was a time of dramatic change in dinghy racing, and sailing generally, as new materials were developed and new techniques were devised to exploit them. Terylene and Dacron were introduced

for sailcloth and lines, and flexible masts and fully-battened mainsails with powerful kicking straps became *de rigueur*. Just having a properly streamlined centreboard could make minutes of difference sailing around a course. Iain rigged and re-rigged *Fantasy* repeatedly, not only ensuring he had a fast boat but also learning vital lessons in aerodynamics.

The juxtaposition of boats and planes may seem a little strange from a sporting point of view, but from a design perspective the two have a great deal in common. Ultimately, one would feed the other in Iain's mind. 'I had a fascination with wings and sails moving through air; the flow of air over an aerofoil shape; how the shapes can vary and what those variations mean. And then there were the interactions of the wings and tails of a plane, like the sails and rudder of a boat; the centreboards and hull; the movement of hull through the water. Boats are more complicated because, between the sea, the wind and the boat, you have an infinite variety of different conditions and things happening. The boat can go in different directions in relation to wind and sea, and the wind and the sea can be doing so many different things.'

This idea was picked up by Iain's brother David, also an accomplished sailor. 'Iain's education in boat design began, I believe, in his early interest in aircraft. Aircraft mandate design efficiency,

Clockwise from top left: Iain's first set of lines became the official plans for the Gwen 12 class; his third Gwen 12 Tuesday; ashore at Mosman Sailing Club. (Photo: courtesy Iain Oughtred.)

especially military aircraft. This was not lost on Iain. More intuitively than by study of the science of aerodynamics, Iain absorbed the profiles of wings, from plan view to cross-section. I remember the rudder design for *Clementine*. Its profile had the shape of a WWII Spitfire wing, unlike the crude original class design. Fuselage construction is all about achieving the greatest strength from the least weight. Look at any of his boat construction details; this is what impresses his admirers and makes his boats stand out from the pack.

'I remember Manfred Curry, one of the first scientists to study the aerodynamics of sails, writing about seeing these aerodynamic shapes in nature, from bird skeletons to windblown sand. I know Iain was familiar with Curry's work, which still stands up today. By making scale models of aircraft designs, and building models that actually flew, I'm sure he absorbed a tremendous amount of this.'

As Iain's default crew ever since the pair of them first started hiring canoes on Balmoral Beach, David also had a rare insight into his approach to racing. 'Compared to many racing sailors, Iain appeared not to be overcome with a competitive need to win,' he says. 'He said that to win a race, all you had to do was just aim the boat. The boat then did the work. It was as though he was flying a sailing boat. He was less interested in the fine art of racing tactics than in feeling the trim of the boat and letting the magic work. It is much easier to win races when you know you have the fastest boat.'

His success with *Clementine* guaranteed Iain orders for more boats, and he went on to build six more Gwen 12s, two for himself and four for other people. He became the official measurer and drew what became the official drawings for the class (subsequently traced by Ken Humphries). It was his first set of drawings and an indication of his increasing interest in boat design. He also acquired himself a new nickname. The day before a championship, he realized that the sail number was missing from one side of his boat's sail, so his crewmate Barry improvised a crude '1516' using black tape. His effort looked more like ISIG than 1516, however, and henceforth Iain became known as 'Isig'. As he says, it was a lucky escape in some ways as it was quite common for skippers to be named after their boats, and Isig was better, on balance, than Clementine.

Iain's success racing and building boats gave his self-confidence a much-needed boost and, as his self-esteem grew, his network of contacts expanded correspondingly. One of his new friends was an up-and-coming designer by the name of Bob Miller (later better known by his adopted name of Ben Lexcen) who in 1983 would break the USA's 132-year domination of the America's Cup with his wing-keeled 12-Metre *Australia II*. When Iain met him, Ben had just designed the 18ft skiff *Taipan*, which in the summer of 1959 sent shockwaves through the fleet due to her narrow, lightweight construction. His next boat, *Venom*, showed him experimenting with a wing centreboard – twenty years before *Australia II*.

Iain met Ben and his business partner Craig Whitworth when he went to the Mosman Sailing Club early one morning to put a coat of varnish on his boat – typically choosing the time when there was least dust and it wasn't too hot. Ben and Craig were snooping about, looking at boats, and struck up a conversation. Ben had yet to make his name in yacht design and was setting up a loft in Sydney. Later, Iain visited the loft at Miller & Whitworth and was invited to work with them making sails. Ben had just designed the Contender, intended as a replacement for the Olympic Finn class, and soon after persuaded Iain to test sail the prototype. Years later, Iain recalled the boat had 'a tendency to twitch to windward to get rid of you, and then attempt to sail away on its own, until capsized by the trapeze wire'.

As for Ben himself, he remembers him as 'an interesting character – a wild man, but a good-hearted guy and a genius'. As their friendship developed and Iain introduced him to his family, he would occasionally come home to find Ben having tea with his mother. He initially assumed that the eccentric designer found Jean's company a refreshing change from the cloak-and-dagger world of the America's Cup, and it was only years later he realized that Ben had his eye on one of Iain's younger sisters.

The most lasting outcome of their meeting was Iain's last – and best – Gwen 12. Keen to promote Miller & Whitworth in the dinghy racing world, Ben offered to donate the sails and rigging if Iain built the fastest boat possible and raced it at the next national championships. *Mary Jane*, subtly tweaked with a ½in flat on the bottom, was one of the most refined Gwen 12s ever built and became something of a legend when she out-foxed the Western Australians at the nationals in Perth in 1963–4.

'It was 2,700 miles away, half of it dirt road, with very fine dust which filled the pot holes so you didn't see them coming. I paid a guy £15 to put the boat on a truck, while my crew Dennis and I went haring off on our own in this amazing old VW. It took us three days and 19 hours, driving an average 40mph for 18 hours a day. We got there totally knackered. The Western Australian sailors were gloating because they didn't think we would be up to the Fremantle Doctor (a strong wind which usually blows up at 3pm). For the first few days, the Doctor didn't come and we had idyllic sailing conditions, much to their annoyance. He finally did come in style on the last day, but *Mary Jane* loved it. Her floppy mast meant we could hold her dead flat on the water, which is what those boats love. We won the championship by the skin of our teeth, and Western Australia was nowhere.'

Mary Jane confirmed Iain's place as the foremost builder and sailor of the class, and her performance would be talked about in racing circles for decades to come.

The growing clarity in his work was matched by a growing certainty in his spiritual beliefs – or, more likely, they both fed each other. In fact, the two strands of his life were not always easy to separate, as he discovered one storm-tossed day crossing the Tasman Sea during the winter of 1978. Iain had joined a friend's 38ft Alden-designed ketch for a cruise to Lord Howe Island, 450 miles northeast of Sydney. On the way, they were hit by a 55-knot storm and the boat went into a broach, throwing the helmsman over the side, only being saved by a rope he had tied to his waist. The four friends patched up the damaged vessel at Lord Howe Island and made their way back to Sydney, only to be hit by more bad weather. In the midst of this drama, which might have put him off sailing for life, Iain had an experience he describes in overtly spiritual terms.

The all-conquering Mary Jane, *on which Iain won the 1964 Gwen 12 National Championship. (Photo: Joy Falls.)*

'While I was on watch, the sun set and put on this fantastic light show – there was every possible cloud and every conceivable shade of every conceivable colour that ever existed. But I had a tremendous feeling of being looked after; that everything was going to be alright and that we were going to make it. There was the feeling of a higher force – without any religious or churchy connotations.

'When you're at sea, you have to come to terms with what you find when you're out there – at whatever level you want. It's an elemental world, stripped to the bone and away from normal life. There are so many levels to engage at and so much to learn. I can't think of any other sport or activity which you can learn so much from. After that experience, I felt a deep down assurance that this was my work – that it was what I was sent here for.'

Despite his success in dinghy racing and despite finally meeting people with whom he shared a common interest, he still felt alienated from the rest of Australian society; as if he was a stranger in his own land. He yearned to visit the land of his forebears. 'I was very much influenced by England when I was young. Our whole culture came from England; the best toys were made there and even our books were published there. By comparison, everything that came from Australia seemed inferior. It was an empty materialistic society. It was as if Australia had grown tired of being British and decided to be American instead.'

He sold *Mary Jane* immediately after the 1964 national championships and, after a few months in Perth, boarded a ship bound for Europe with his friend Mike Lyndon-James (otherwise known as 'Mouse'). They had no idea how long they were going for but, in his heart of hearts, Iain hoped he would never go back again.

Iain's eventful voyage to Lord Howe Island earned a mention in the Sydney Morning Herald.

IAIN ON FULL-LENGTH BATTENS

(Extract from *WoodenBoat* July/August 1987)

An aerodynamically efficient type of conventional sail has full-length battens that can support a roach of up to one third of the sail's total area. Sailors brought up on full-length battens find it difficult to understand why they are not more popular. A battened sail holds its shape better in use, and the battens act as 'racing stripes', making it easy to read the sail's shape. Their effect in quieting a luffing sail is appreciated in heavy weather. If the boat is caught in a sudden hard squall, when the whole sail must be eased, the battens can actually save her from capsizing; a wildly flogging 'soft' sail has a lot of drag – as well as an inclination to tear itself apart.

Luffing when sailing close-hauled, for which the racing sailor is watching constantly, is a little less apparent, but visible enough if the battens are not too closely spaced. We used to think we needed at least nine battens, and some sails had a dozen or more, but seven now seems to be about the usual number in smaller sails.

A fully battened sail can approximate the ideal elliptical plan form that the aerodynamicists have found gives the best lift-to-drag ratios over a wide range of conditions. C A Marchaj, in his *Aero-Hydrodynamics of Sailing*, concludes that in many conditions even square-headed sails – trapezoidal or rectangular – can be at least theoretically superior to the highly-tapered basic Bermudian form. He argues that rating rules, in limiting headboard width and upper sail chord dimensions, restrict experimentation that could lead to more effective sail plans than the conventional three-cornered type. However, the respected author does not detail some practical problems such as the weight, drag, and structural complications of gaffs and strongly curved spars. His implication is clear, though: the narrow, pointed head of a tall sail, with the turbulence of the mast before it, probably causes more drag than lift in most situations. The fully battened sail largely eliminates this ineffective narrow corner by increasing the angle between the luff and the leech.

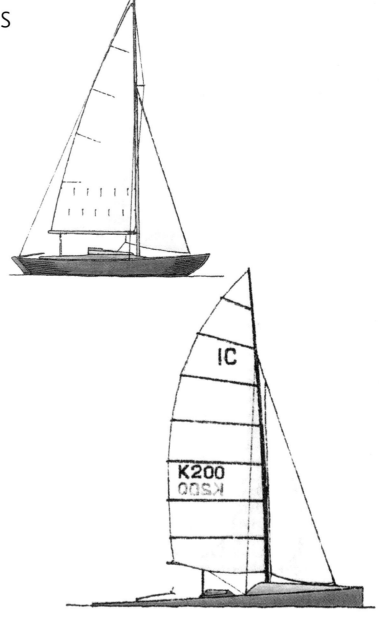

Full-length battens are more work to make, and more costly, than leech battens, but only minimal extra work is needed to make the sail for them – less work is needed, in fact, if the sail is cut so that the seams overlap about 2in to form the batten pockets, leaving no seams between the battens. Full-length battens are no more trouble to look after and are generally left in the sail when the boat is unrigged. The sail need only be rolled up around them, sometimes around the boom as well, and stored in a long, thin bag. This is better for the sail than folding it into a small sail bag.

chapter 2
NEW BEGINNINGS

THE SIXTIES REVOLUTION was just getting under way when Iain arrived in London in August 1964. A Labour government headed by Harold Wilson had just been elected to power with a slim majority, which would be consolidated at the next election. A range of liberal social policies was about to be introduced, from the abolition of the death penalty to the legalisation of male homosexuality and the liberalization of abortion laws. Thanks to Mary Quant, London had taken over from Paris as the centre of the fashion world and Beatlemania was at its peak, with 'Can't Buy Me Love', 'A Hard Day's Night' and 'I Feel Fine' all hitting the No 1 spot that year.

After five weeks at sea, the Greek liner docked in Piraeus and Iain and Mouse set foot for the first time on European soil. A crowded train journey across Italy and Switzerland took them to Calais, where they boarded a ferry to England. Once in London, like many Australian ex-pats before and after them, they found a variety of casual jobs, including washing cars, working at the Army & Navy department store and, in Iain's case, teaching English at a French private school in Worcestershire, before eventually settling on driving vans. It wasn't building boats and it wasn't near the sea, but it did give Iain a chance to travel around Britain and see what the country was like. It was the beginning of a love affair with what was to become his adopted land.

'As soon as I got to Britain, I knew this was where I wanted to live. I had no intention of going back to Australia,' he says. 'I bought a Lambretta scooter and drove all around town on it. It was autumn and London was beautiful. I was impressed rather than appalled by the cold. When we were driving the vans, we arrived at the depot in Harrow while it was still dark. We stood about as it was beginning to get light, blowing WD-40 over the engines to get them started. I had a fantasy the vans were a bunch of Lancasters [aircraft] and we were about to take off on some great expedition. When we were done, we'd race back to the depot and swap stories about the daft people we'd met.'

It was near the end of this first visit to Britain that Iain made a trip that would, ultimately, change his life. Mouse's girlfriend came over from California to visit, and the three of them set off in an old Land Rover to visit Scotland; Mouse and Debbie staying in smart hotels, while Iain roughed it in the back of the car. It was January and the landscape was bleak and cold, but it spoke to Iain in a way nowhere had before.

BELOW *Living in London in the late 1960s, Iain earned his crust making dulcimers. (Photo: courtesy Iain Oughtred.)*

'I totally fell in love with Scotland. I believed this was my place, where I should be. I felt a deep down connection, like an empathy with my ancestral roots,' he says. 'I felt much the same way as when I had first arrived in England, and just felt very comfortable being there. Whenever I spent time away and came back to London, I loved hearing people speak; just hearing English accents was comforting. But I felt the Scots had a bit more initiative, more enterprise, and were more open and friendly – because London, as I discovered, could be a very lonely place. After that first trip, I was ready to pack up the Lambretta and head up to Edinburgh.'

It was not to be. When he returned to London, Iain received news from home telling him that his father had died. Within a few days, he had forsaken the mixed blessings of a British spring for the tail end of an Australian summer. It would be another 23 years before he finally moved north to his 'ancestral' home of Scotland.

Although he had spent most of his life in Australia and held an Australian passport, when he returned to the land of his birth in 1966, Iain felt no sense of 'homecoming'. Far from it. He felt as if he had been wrenched from his real home and dragged back to a foreign land. His time away from Australia had confirmed something he had felt very profoundly since he was a small child: he didn't belong in this place. He later expressed the sentiment in suitably nautical terms to an American boating magazine: 'Just because you were born on a ship in the ocean, that doesn't mean that is where you belong. Australia was my ship in the ocean.'

He returned to find his mother in a process of transition. No longer beholden to her charismatic but domineering husband, she was free to do whatever she wanted to do. 'For 30 years she had been totally unable to make any decision for herself and had just got on and looked after the kids,' he remembers. 'Finally, after Dad died, she had a bit of freedom, and started doing all sorts of things she had never been able to do before. She went to art classes and yoga, and met all sorts of interesting people. For years, she had been listening to the Beatles, the Rolling Stones and Bob Dylan and thinking, these guys have got some interesting things to say – the times they are a-changing. And she perceived that that really was dead right, because things really were changing.'

The times were a-changing for Iain too. Soon after arriving in Australia, he got a job as a draughtsman at the office of Cecil E Boden and Associates in Sydney. The company specialized in commercial craft, such as tugs and trawlers, as well as small motor cruisers. Although Iain had virtually no experience of draughtsmanship, apart from drawing the Gwen 12 plans for the class association six years earlier, Cecil Boden were impressed by his enthusiasm and his general boating knowledge and set him to work on the company's stock plans. He started work there, memorably, on 6 June, or 6/6/66.

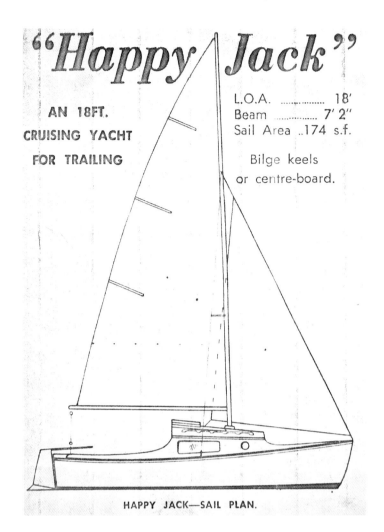

"Happy Jack"

AN 18FT. CRUISING YACHT FOR TRAILING

L.O.A. .... 18'
Beam .... 7' 2"
Sail Area ..174 s.f.

Bilge keels
or centre-board.

HAPPY JACK—SAIL PLAN.

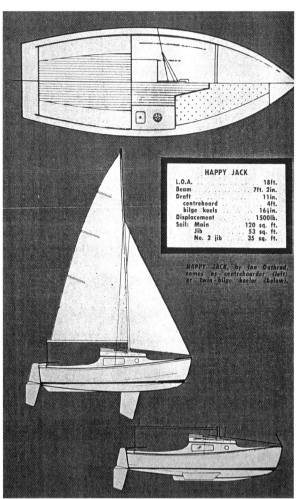

HAPPY JACK

L.O.A.	18ft.
Beam	7ft. 2in.
Draft	11in.
centreboard	4ft.
bilge keels	16½in.
Displacement	1500lb.
Sail: Main	120 sq. ft.
Jib	53 sq. ft.
No. 2 jib	35 sq. ft.

HAPPY JACK, by Ian Outhred, comes as centreboarder (left) or twin-bilge keeler (below).

It was while he was working at Boden's that Iain designed his first boat. The Happy Jack was an 18ft hard-chine pocket cruiser inspired by the *Yachting World* Senior. She probably looked much like any other pocket cruiser on Sydney Harbour, although there is a sureness of touch about her that suggests her designer knew exactly what he was trying to achieve and how to achieve it. She was offered with the option of bermudan or gunter rig and with either centreboard or bilge keels. Two bunks, a galley and a heads area were packed into her fulsome hull. Iain's attention to detail was already evident in the profile drawings, with the cabin sides neatly extended fore and aft to create cockpit and foredeck coamings.

The boat was aimed at the amateur builder with a middle to low income who, in the words of a review in *Modern Boating* magazine in July 1967, 'wants to keep the boat at home and save on the cost of mooring'. To make them suitable for homebuilding, the plans had to include a level of detail not required by a professional boatbuilder, and from the outset Iain seemed particularly good at this aspect of the job. His own experience as a boatbuilder helped him anticipate which aspects of the construction process the novice might find difficult and to provide the necessary information. On a deeper level, he himself had struggled so much with education that he had an empathy with the amateur, struggling to get a foothold on the 'system' – any system.

The *Modern Boating* article duly notes that 'Ian Outhred [sic] is himself a meticulous boatbuilder, and he has prepared a list of detailed but simple instructions to help amateurs with little or no experience in boatbuilding.'

Designed in 1966/67, Happy Jack was the first Oughtred design to be published. Several plans were sold, and at least one boat built.

As for the boat's name, it was inspired by a single released in 1966 by the British rock band The Who. 'Happy Jack' was a surreal song about a man who 'lived in the sand at the Isle of Man' and was teased by children playing on the beach. It includes the suitably watery lyrics:

'But they couldn't stop Jack, or the waters lapping
And they couldn't prevent Jack from feeling happy.'

Iain confesses to not knowing what the song was about, and apparently Mr Boden never asked, but the name stuck none the less.

Despite his natural talent for technical drawing, most of his work at Boden's proved to be pretty mundane and, after a year of it, he grew bored with, as he puts it, 'drawing engine bearers in motor cruisers'. A few years earlier, while taking part in the C Class catamaran trials in Victoria, he had met Bob Ross, the editor of *Modern Boating* magazine, and the pair struck up an unlikely friendship. When the magazine decided to start selling boat plans, Bob immediately thought of Iain and invited him to run the service. It was a dream job for a cerebral boat nut and brought Iain into contact with many of the top designers of the day in Australia, including the celebrated Len Hedges, who was, says Iain, 'the only man I ever deliberately got drunk with'.

With the increased availability of plywood and better adhesives, amateur boatbuilding took off dramatically after the war and, for the first time, sailing became a sport of the masses. *Modern Boating* had been founded on the back of this phenomenon, and a mail order service for amateur plans was a logical extension of their work. The magazine's new venture was unveiled to the world in the September 1967 issue and featured designs by John Spencer, Richard Hartley, Lock Crowther and Len Hedges. The article included an introduction to its latest new member of staff, which put an upbeat spin on his two years odd-jobbing in Britain: 'To head our plans department, we have appointed a keen sailor, experienced in boatbuilding, drafting and designing. He is Ian Outhred [sic], who was Australian Gwen 12 class champion in 1961–62, 1963–64. Ian recently returned to Australia after two years in England, where he studied boat trends.'

Bob Ross, who went on to found the successful *Australian Sailing* magazine, remembers those days with affection: 'Ian [sic] was good at the job, with his practical experience as a boatbuilder and design knowledge. Bearded, easy-going, imbued with the spirit of the Swinging Sixties he had enjoyed in Britain, he fitted in socially with the staff and was popular with the customers. In those days we occupied an ancient, small building in Lower Bathurst Street; an area since demolished to make way for a road-system flyover. Colin Ryrie and Jules Feldman [the owners of *Modern Boating*], on moving into the building, established a bar in its cellar, for entertaining clients as an amenity to the staff who would meet there for after-work drinks. We had some big, happy parties there, but it also became a bit of a trap with unannounced visitors expecting to be entertained by other members of the staff if Col or Jules were not around. The advertising manager for one of the biggest outboard motor companies would drop in at opening time with a bottle of milk, looking for a Bundaberg rum to go to make the famed "Moreton Bay porridge".'

Meanwhile, Iain was racing his beloved Gwen 12s again, including taking part in the nationals at Botany Bay in Sydney, when he literally sailed the bottom off a boat that started delaminating in a 'Southerly Buster'. He had also overcome his chronic shyness enough to get himself a girlfriend – although, as neither of them were particularly 'happy jacks', the relationship soon turned into an emotional rollercoaster. The couple had already separated when Carrie announced that she was pregnant with Iain's child. They managed to get back together, partly at the instigation of Iain's mother Jean, but it was not to last. Haig Conolly Outhred was born on 11 January 1968 and, after another attempt to patch things up, Iain left after a month without even having unpacked his bags. For the next twenty years, the only news he would have of his son was via his mother Jean, who was allowed to see Haig on the strict condition that Iain wasn't told of his whereabouts. It was a painful experience and one that would make him wary of entering into any meaningful relationships in the future.

Still reeling from this bruising encounter and not feeling any more at ease in Australia than he had before his first visit to Europe, he decided it was time to escape – back to England. Another seven-week voyage saw him back in London, where he found a place to stay on the top floor of a house on East Heath Road, overlooking Hampstead Heath, in one of the leafiest and most pleasant parts of the city. He was keen to continue with his boat design work and, thanks to his connection with Bob Ross, found openings with two of Britain's leading designers: Roderick MacAlpine Downie and Robert Tucker. He soon realized, however, that he had no affinity with the big, heavy cruising catamarans that he was being asked to draw and he returned to his old job of driving vans around London for Gentle Ghost, an alternative employment agency.

It was 1968, and Britain was in the throes of the Summer of Love. Everyone knew that the discredited and outmoded world order was about to collapse, and there was no point in developing a 'proper' career. Iain made leather bags to sell on Portobello Road, grew his hair long, listened to folk music and practised transcendental meditation. In short, he became a hippy. 'It was a good time because there was a feeling of possibility; that people might be able to live together in peace and harmony and not rip each other off; that everything was going to be alright. It was a universal thing. People would recognize each other in the street and smile spontaneously, and people would smile back, and you knew that they knew. It was enormously refreshing.'

But, however much of a hippy he tried to be, Iain's religious upbringing was never far away. His enforced attendance at Sunday school and countless communions may not have taught him to become a conventionally upstanding member of society, but they did imbue him with a strong sense of the spiritual. His religious background also helped him see through the materialistic society which he had been brought up in and to have a healthy disregard for material possessions – something reinforced by his own necessarily frugal lifestyle. What he lacked, however, was a focus for his spiritual impulse.

The solution, when it came, presented itself without his having to look for it. While he was living in Hampstead, he frequently passed the Quaker Meeting House on Heath Street and became intrigued by its stylized Arts and Crafts architecture. Built in 1907, the building was designed by Frederick Rowntree, of the famous Quaker chocolate manufacturing family, who was responsible for a great many of the Friends Meeting Houses around Britain. Eventually, Iain plucked up the courage to go inside and was surprised by the welcome he received.

'I was of quite an alternative appearance at that time – fairly hairy, with the beads and patched up old jeans,' he remembers. 'I was quite accustomed to the idea that this was something different to respectable society and sometimes not approved of. But there was no sense of judgment at the Meeting House. The people there were relaxed and friendly in a genuine way, not just for the sake of being welcoming. I could have been wearing a suit and tie, and I would have received exactly the same welcome.'

With its lack of religious symbolism and its long history of pacifism, Quakerism offered a relatively neutral outlet for the spiritual feelings he had nurtured all his adult life – a simple conviction that there was a higher force out there, albeit without the churchy connotations of his Presbyterian upbringing. It was also a loose enough affiliation that would allow him to float in and out as his mood took him, without judging him by the number of times he had or hadn't been to a meeting. It also gave him a worldwide network of contacts that would prove extremely useful in years to come.

Meanwhile, Iain was determined to see a bit more of the world. In 1970, he flew to New York and then Montreal, where he bought a BSA 250 motorbike and embarked on a classic Easy Rider-style journey across America. Compared to his old Lambretta, the BSA looked great and made all the right noises, but it was completely inadequate for the task in hand and broke a pushrod 31 miles out of Winnipeg, halfway across Canada's border with the USA. He eventually made it to Vancouver where, after making leather bags and belts to raise money, he swapped the bike for a VW and headed south to California. There, he learned that the spirit of peace and love hadn't quite prevailed when he was arrested for making a wrong turn in his VW or, as he puts it, for 'looking at a policeman the wrong way'. He spent Christmas Eve in a prison cell in Berkeley, mulling over the fact that, of 13 people in his cell, all but one were either black or had long hair.

'It was a shocking experience, but it gave an interesting insight into how it can be to be the wrong kind of person in the wrong place at the wrong time, ie black, Indian, Jewish. Or a "freak",' Iain remembers. 'But I loved the people in America – the right sort of people – and their way of life. The whole spectacularly creative Love and Peace transformation that seemed to be happening was so wonderfully expressed in the music of the time. I was struck by the general intuitive sensitivity to the state of the earth and the increasing urgency to treat it with due respect.'

Back in Europe, he carried on with his peripatetic lifestyle, modelling for art classes at ten bob an hour, working as a 'man with a (VW) van' in London, visiting friends in Amsterdam and attending transcendental meditation courses in Switzerland and France. While he was in California, he had built himself a dulcimer, and he now acquired a 12in bandsaw and started building the instruments in earnest, delighting at the variety of shapes and sizes he was able to achieve. Over the next few years, he built and sold 49 in total – a tribute to his craftsmanship and meticulous attention to detail.

It was on a trip to France that a friend gave him a copy of L Francis Herreshoff's 1946 book *The Common Sense of Yacht Design*. Included alongside a discussion of rarefied topics such as cabin arrangements, marine hardware and measurement rules, were a selection of Herreshoff's own designs – impossibly romantic boats such as the *Bounty*, *Tioga* and *Araminta*, as well as more accessible yachts such as the *H28* and *Nereia*. Iain read the book from cover to cover once and then read it all over again. Suddenly, after years of stumbling from one job to the next, it became clear to him: he had to be a boat designer.

His new resolve was strengthened when, in 1972–3, he drove with a couple of friends across Scandinavia, starting in Denmark before crossing to Sweden and then Norway. While the others were admiring the scenery and the architecture, Iain was fascinated by the double-ended workboats he saw dragged up on the foreshore or being rowed across the fjords. He photographed them almost obsessively and made rough pencil sketches, which, at night, he turned into ink drawings by candlelight in the back of the van. Towards the end of the journey, he visited the Viking Ship Museum in Oslo, which he describes as 'the most astonishing thing I'd ever seen'. Occupying a cross-shaped building of a quasi-spiritual character, the museum houses three boats excavated from separate graves in Norway, the most spectacular being the highly decorated Oseberg ship,

dating from AD820. He would later describe the vessel as a work of art which deserved to be ranked alongside Chartres Cathedral and Beethoven's symphonies.

But, although he now started sketching designs and reading about the subject in earnest, actually breaking into the sailing world in Britain – let alone becoming a designer – proved as elusive as ever. He was too much of a rebel to fit in with the blue-blazered yachty brigade, while the dinghy racing world was too highly competitive and the traditional wooden boat scene virtually non-existent. Once again, it wasn't until he went back 'down under' that his first break came.

Iain returned to Australia in 1974 for no particular reason, other than a 'feeling' that he should go, only to discover when he got there that his mother was having a stroke and being rushed to hospital. Fortuitously, Iain had turned up at just the right time to help nurse her back to health and spend a little time getting to know her. The result was a wonderful and unbargained for deepening of their relationship which would continue to develop, albeit usually at some distance apart, until her death several years later.

His visit was auspicious from a professional point of view too, as a few months later he received his first design commission. Jan de Voogd, a fellow Quaker at the Sydney Meeting House, wanted Iain to build him a 28–30ft bilge-keeled cruising yacht and asked him to help him choose a design. After talking to several designers and not finding anything he liked, Jan realized that Iain had a better grasp of the kind of boat he wanted than any of the professionals and asked him to come up with a suitable design. The result was the 29ft *Duyfken*, officially design No 6, which Iain helped build in 1976–7. His old friend Len Hedges went over the design and made sure his calculations were correct, while boatbuilder Rob Crosby oversaw the construction of the boat.

Norway's double-enders made a lasting impression on Iain when he visited Scandinavia in the early 1970s. (Photo: Iain Oughtred.)

The design was an unusual mix of old and new, with a cut away forefoot and large skeg, combined with a traditional double-ended hull and raised foredeck. Cold-moulded out of Tasmanian cedar and glued together with resorcinol, the hull was fitted out using local timbers such as King William pine and celery top (a tough timber similar to the famous Huon pine). The yacht went on to do some serious voyaging around the east coast of Australia, including a hairy passage across the infamous Bass Strait in 55 knots of wind with an unreefed mainsail. It was one of the few times the spray reached the cockpit.

While in Australia, Iain started work on another project that would turn into an important landmark: his first Moth design. He had long had an interest in the class and had watched its extraordinary development with an avid eye. He had noticed, however, that although there were a number of designs on the market for amateur construction, there were few available of the popular 'scow-bowed' type. He set about to rectify this situation with his Fish design, which was a development of his own boat *Earwig*. He built the prototype himself, photographing every stage, and wrote the process up in a series of articles published by *Australian Sailing* magazine – which his friend Bob Ross had launched two years earlier – in May to August 1978, including a history of the class since 1928.

In the second article, he describes his objectives as follows: 'Firstly, to work out a design which truly represents the "state of the art", a hull of moderate proportions and no unproven peculiarities, a boat which should look as good as any if built right, and stay together for a few seasons if looked after. Secondly, I want to provide a really complete plan, including details of spars and all the bits and pieces, as well as sufficient information to enable anyone with reasonable woodworking ability to put together a fair and a complete and competitive outfit using either bought or home-made sails and spars. A complete list of materials, rigging and fittings will be included.'

At the end of the article, the Fish plans are listed for sale at AUS$20 a set, and an address at Glover Street, Mosman NSW 2088 is given as his contact. It was the first Outhred/Oughtred dinghy available for public consumption and, while not proving a best-seller, provided a template for not only designing and building his own designs, but also marketing them. For, in his own roundabout way, Iain was homing in on what would become his life's mission: designing good boats for amateur construction, or what a colleague of his would later describe as 'beautiful boats for the masses'. Although his mission statement was only directed at the Moth, it would come in time to have a much wider application and, indeed, could be read as a manifesto for all his future work.

But although Iain knew what he wanted to do, he hadn't yet found the right medium to express himself. Because he didn't come from a family with any maritime tradition, his boating knowledge was limited to what he had stumbled across on Sydney Harbour or read about in books. He would come to envy designers such as Paul Gartside, who had been brought up in boatyards seeing boats being built day in and day out, and who had built up such an affinity with the subject that designing them was almost second nature. By contrast, Iain had had no formal training and had no personal boating heritage to fall back on. What maritime heritage was available to him in Australia was limited to contemporary racing dinghies and traditional craft mostly imported from the Old World.

But Iain was an avaricious reader. Years earlier, he had devoured a borrowed stack of old *Rudder* magazines from the 1940s and 1950s, when L Francis Herreshoff was still a regular contributor, and he had fallen in love with Herreshoff's style in *The Common Sense of Yacht Design*. As he read more widely, he became immersed in the work of Howard Chapelle, Phil Bolger, Pete Culler, John Gardner, Robert Clark and Laurent Giles. Because most of the available literature on traditional boat types came from the USA, most of what he read was about American indigenous craft, detailing the development of boats such as the Grand Bank dories and the New Haven sharpies.

Back in Britain, his Quaker network came up trumps and he got a bursary to spend three terms at the Quaker Study Centre at Woodbrooke near Birmingham, studying photography, music and calligraphy, as well as theology and the history of Quakerism. In his spare time, he drew several new designs, including a 25ft sloop and 38ft clipper-bowed ketch clearly inspired by

ABOVE *Iain the intellectual; studying at the Woodbrook Quaker Study Centre, near Birmingham. (Photo: courtesy Iain Oughtred.)*

OPPOSITE, TOP *Iain's first design commission was unlike anything that followed: the 29ft long keel cutter* Duyfken. *(Photo: Iain Oughtred.)*

OPPOSITE, BOTTOM Duyfken *was cold-moulded out of Tasmanian cedar. (Photo: Jan de Voogd.)*

Herreshoff – although the nearest either design got to being launched was in the form of two half-models he built while he was at Woodbrook. As well as being intellectually and creatively stimulating, it was a sociable time and allowed him to experience another community very different to the testosterone-fuelled Australian boating scene.

For, despite his introverted nature, Iain seemed to crave being part of a community, whether it was through the hippy movement, transcendental meditation, Quakerism or, later, the various alternative groups he would be repeatedly drawn to through his peripatetic lifestyle. On a psychological level, you could say he was seeking a family to replace the family he never really felt a part of, or a society to replace the society he never really felt he belonged to. Or you could just say he was trying to find his place in the world.

In 1981 he visited the United States again and witnessed for himself the extraordinary revival of interest in traditional wooden boats, particularly on the East Coast. He went to the offices of *WoodenBoat* magazine and met designers and builders such as Damian McLaughlin, Dick Newick and Walter Green. He even made contact with Phil Bolger, one of the leading lights of the American wooden boat revival, and asked if he could visit him. The great man's reply was characteristically forthright.

'He told me he charged US$30 per hour for consultations. I was a bit surprised, but I told him I'd think about it. I suppose, being that well known and accessible, he was being hassled infinitely. After a while, I thought I'd probably get US$30's worth of information and rang him to make an appointment. In the end, I spent about 2½ hours with him and got more than my money's worth. I'd done very little myself by that time, but I showed him pictures of what I'd done, and he said, "You've got some good stuff here." I said, "I'm glad you think so," – as I really was – and he said: "It's not an opinion, it's a fact." He let me park my VW bus in his driveway overnight, which was handy, but I didn't see him again in the morning.'

Soon after, he was introduced to British designer Nigel Irens, soon to make his mark on the multihull racing circuit with designs such as Tony Bullimore's *Apricot*, the legendary *ENZA*, and, perhaps most famously, Ellen MacArthur's record-breaking *B&Q*. Nigel was still relatively unknown when Iain met him and, like Iain, deliberately set himself outside the establishment. Iain was looking for somewhere to stay and, with characteristic generosity, Nigel offered him his flat in Bristol while he was away for a few weeks. The few weeks turned into months and then nearly two years after Nigel returned and invited Iain to stay on in the spare room. Iain acted as a sounding board while Nigel was working up his ideas for Bullimore's trimaran, and built a prototype model to see how the evolving shape would look.

'Iain was that rare thing: a quiet Australian,' remembers Nigel. 'He was someone who was not afraid to leave an awkward silence – even on the telephone – where most people would rush to fill the void. It could be disquieting if you were not used to it. He was involved in his work at a very deep level and made it an integral part of his life, something which is rare to see these days. I don't think his lack of formal training was a barrier. Too much education can be stultifying and puts you on the same rails as everyone else. Freedom of thought has served both of us quite well.

'Something we had in common was that we had our education in many fields, which was quite rare at that time. Like him, I was happy doing dinghies, trimarans or traditional boats. In recent years, it's become clear that they all linked parts of a bigger subject, and that if you constrain yourself to one camp, you won't have the full range of experiences. The progress of textiles, for example, means they can now be used in a racing context. Using rope instead of

turnbuckles, as I have done on several high-tech racers, is a traditional solution to a modern rigging problem. That's how the different technologies feed off each other.'

As if to prove the point, while he was living in Bristol, Iain won recognition for two very contemporary-looking cruising yachts: one a two-masted unstayed ketch, which was ranked among the top three in a *Yachting World* design competition; the other a 40ft fin-keeled sloop that received an Honourable Mention in a *Cruising World* competition. He also drew a 30ft trimaran and built a scale model of it which he tested to death in Bristol harbour. Big boats and small boats, race boats and cruising boats; all fed his growing fascination with the dynamics of hull and sail design.

Iain's first venture into the idiom of traditional boat design was, not surprisingly, heavily influenced by the mass of literature he had absorbed about American working boats. And what could be more quintessentially American than a dory? The Blackfish was a 15ft 4in 'light dory', not dissimilar to Phil Bolger's hugely popular Gloucester Gull, but with lapstrake sides and a more traditional appearance. With straight sides and a flat bottom, it was an easy boat to build, either in plywood or solid timber, and came with the option of a daggerboard and a simple bermudan rig. Iain built the prototype at a workshop he rented at the docks, using plywood and resorcinol glue, a technology which had served him well in the past.

Having built the boat, he was then able to go back to his drawings, adjust them as necessary and add the nitty gritty details needed by the amateur builder. He then had his first set of

Iain settles into his new home, sailing a traditionally-built coble in the Bristol Channel. (Photo: courtesy Iain Oughtred.)

ABOVE *The launch of a new career: building the Blackfish dory in Bristol in 1981. (Photo: Iain Oughtred.)*

RIGHT *Right from the beginning, Iain liked to build his designs wherever possible, to iron out any problems. (Photo: Iain Oughtred.)*

traditional boat plans available for public consumption – plans that are still available in his catalogue. He put an ad in the back of *Practical Boat Owner* magazine offering them for sale at £15, and gradually the orders started coming in. It was only about one sale a week to start with, but it was enough to suggest that, if he could design more boats and develop a full range of designs, he could make a living from it.

While he was in Bristol, Iain consolidated his links with the Old Country by researching his family history at the local library. He discovered that the usual spelling of his family name was Oughtred – not Outhred as he had been christened – and was derived from the medieval words for dusk/dawn/half-light (from 'uht') and counsellor (from 'reed' or 'red'). Subsequent research revealed that the name is mentioned in the Doomsday book of 1088 and twice before that. His research suggested that the name was most common in Yorkshire, Northumberland, Oxfordshire and the West Country, although there were also half a dozen references to it in Scotland as well. Notable Oughtreds included Sir Anthony Ughtred (a 16th-century spelling of the name) who was married to Elizabeth Seymour, sister of Henry VIII's third wife Jane Seymour, and William Oughtred, who invented the slide rule. There was also Thomas Oughtred, who was in the court of Edward II and who, much to Iain's chagrin, advised him in a famous victory over the Scots.

ABOVE *Ever a supporter of rowing, Iain gets to grips with the newly-launched Blackfish dory. (Photo: courtesy Iain Oughtred.)*

Part of the Oughtred family ended up in Ireland, from where they emigrated to Australia in 1853. There was an even stronger Celtic link on his mother's side of the family, the Hendersons, who came from Orkney at the northern tip of Scotland. A branch of the family emigrated in the late 1800s, when one brother moved to Glasgow to become a moderator for the Church of Scotland and the other took a ship to Australia.

At the age of 42, Iain was reconnecting with his roots at every level. And, increasingly, he would remain in Britain, travelling ever further north in an apparent quest for those Scottish ancestors. It was as if he was possessed by a disgruntled Celtic spirit which had never wanted to leave Britain and needed to return there to find peace. As his brother David put it, 'Iain's move back to first England and then Scotland was an expression of his rejection of the consumer/materialist culture that continues to overwhelm Australia. He needed to connect more directly with social elements that reflected tradition and respect for craftsmanship, natural materials and folk culture.'

To mark this new chapter in his life he did a symbolic thing: he changed his name. He reverted to the old spelling of Oughtred and adopted the Celtic spelling of his first name, which was in any case how his mother Jean had originally envisioned it. Thus, the Australian dinghy racer Ian Outhred became the British (and ultimately Scottish) boat designer Iain Oughtred. It was the beginning of a new life.

IAIN ON MAKING A MOTH

(Extract from *Australian Sailing*, May 1978)

Someone once said that a sailing boat is more like a living thing than any of man's creations. Certainly the Moth is very much like a live creature – sometimes like a mad thing! – and she is very demanding. The skipper must become part of the machine, refining his technique so that he can instantly respond to her slightest whim, to be firm yet gentle at the same time so as to keep her always moving at top speed. He must be very quick and positive in his movements, and move lightly so as not to fall through the floor.

Nearly all top skippers now are young guys between about 21 to 26, with quite a few seasons' experience. A reasonably competent skipper from another class may be dismayed to find he cannot get away with anything: a moment's inattention or an imperfect tack and the boat just falls over (I speak from experience!).

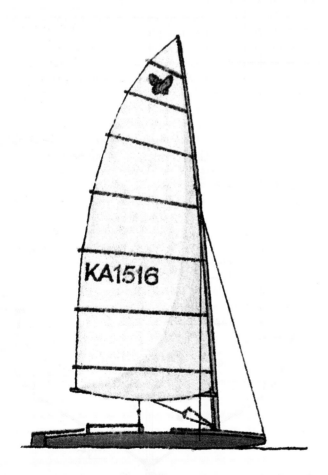

But the rewards are worthwhile: to plane lightly past an Eight Metre with her huge spinnaker drawing; to surf along the wake of a powerboat; to know the pure sensation of sailing in a boat so light that she can be unloaded from a car, rigged and launched single-handed.

Although you are so close to the water, she is not a very wet boat to sail; the scow bow does not throw much spray at you, and on the wings you are clear of most of it anyway. But occasionally she will sail through a wave instead of over it, stagger a bit, shake herself and leap away again. [...]

The Moth offers a refreshing and necessary alternative to the modern tendency towards mass produced boats. Nobody has been able to build a fibreglass hull light and stiff enough; most boats are home-built and maintained. I want to take it a step further, by setting out the details of construction, spar- and sailmaking etc, so that a newcomer to the class can put together a sound and competitive boat without the lumps and bumps which show up many amateur hulls.

If one has the time, a lot of money can be saved; the Moth Association says it will cost AUS$600 to AUS$700 to build a boat with all the go-fast gear, or AUS$1200 to finish a professionally-built hull. My boat *Earwig* cost around AUS$400 in the water and by buying just the right gear first time I could now build a better boat for AUS$350. Not bad for a top-class international racing yacht! She seems to be as quick as any in most conditions, if only her skipper can clean up his act a bit and so give her a chance to prove it.

I am not insisting that everyone does it this way; a lot of people are not able to take six weeks off to build a boat. But I believe it is a valid approach and offer it for what it is worth. The sailmaker can sell you an immaculate sail with a predictable performance; the home-made sail will teach you a lot about sailmaking and enable you to make any adjustments you like to the shape of it. The sailmakers should thank me for that at least.

An alloy mast costs AUS$85 to AUS$110, or if you

have a couple of days to spare and a lot of clamps, you can buy a piece of oregon for about AUS$16.50 and learn about sparmaking and get a spar which should be lighter, and probably work as well, or if not, can fairly easily be modified to suit crew weight and sail shape.

A history of the class would just about represent a history of the evolution of racing centreboard boat development. The Moth was a pioneer in lightweight construction, high-ratio fully-battened sails, deck-stepped and rotating masts, transom-draining cockpits and fully-adjustable rigs.

The class started way back in 1928, when Len Morris built his *Olive*, a simple flat bottomed scow, and made such an impression that a number of clubs in Victoria were soon sailing similar boats. In 1933 the Moth became a recognized class. Similar boats were being built to roughly the same basic restrictions in America from 1930, and in England from 1936; all were called Moths, but it was not until 1968 that the rules of the Australian class were accepted as the basis for the International Moth Class [...]

The Moth still offers a lot of scope for inventiveness but the newcomer to the class is well advised not to let his imagination run riot if he wants a fast boat with good resale value. My own *Earwig* is perhaps a good example: I started from the Snubby

plan, added a 'normal' bow a little hollowed, and a wider, lower chine aft which made her very similar to Ian Brown's latest hulls.

But, thinking that with the deep bow and flat run the boat should go better backwards, I flattened the entry a little (actually ⅜in at mast-bulkhead area) and gave her a little more rocker aft. She just would not stay with them in any conditions and after chopping the rig around every other week, in desperation I ripped half the bottom off and added ⅜in to the bottom of the transom, fairing in chines and stringers so that the run was now the same as the Snubby from the bulkhead aft. This transformed the performance and she now seems fast on all points, especially downwind. But she nosedives fairly readily, having reduced buoyancy forward and I thought that a fuller bow would be better in open water. [...]

I would like to see someone build an 'easy' boat. A large proportion of skippers are not getting the best out of their boats, partly through lack of experience, and I feel that many of them would be better off with a more stable hull a few inches wider, and a lower rig: shorter luff and less roach that would be more easily balanced and controlled. They would have an easier and more enjoyable time, need rescuing less often, and actually go faster, being more in control of the situation.

chapter 3
THE DESIGNER AS ARTIST

Iain rows the prototype Acorn Skiff, the boat that launched his career, on the upper reaches of the Thames. (Photo: courtesy Iain Oughtred.)

T'S USUALLY DIFFICULT, if not impossible, to pinpoint the precise starting point of a movement – be it a major social upheaval, such as the civil rights movement in the US in the 1960s, or minor social trends, such as the fad for flared or baggy or skinny jeans. In the case of the wooden boat revival, you could point to the Antique Boat Show in Clayton, New York in 1965, or the formation of the Old Gaffers Association in Britain in 1958. But while these events showed a growing awareness of traditional craft in general, there were still precious few new wooden boats being built in the US until the 'revival proper' took off in the 1970s. In Britain, the movement was even slower to get going, with wooden boatbuilding being essentially moribund throughout the 1960s and 70s.

That was all to change over the following two decades, and the source of that change can at least in part be traced back to a cold, draughty shed in Cookham Dean on the River Thames. There, during the winter of 1981–2, Iain built his first Acorn Skiff. Like his Blackfish Dory, the design was inspired by traditional American craft – this time the exquisite Whitehall dinghy, revered across the United States. One of the first boats to be produced *en masse*, the Whitehall was the ultimate 'water taxi' of the 1800s and was known for its ability to ferry goods and people across a harbour at speed. With its fine lines and wineglass stern, it was also strikingly beautiful and is still rightly venerated in US maritime folklore. The boat that Iain drew was at the smaller end of the type, and was correspondingly fuller, with a slightly larger transom than the typical Whitehall.

But the biggest difference was the construction method. Like Iain's dory, the Acorn Skiff was to be built out of plywood, but whereas the planks on the dory were glued together with resorcinol glue, this time Iain decided to try out the new wonder glue that everybody was talking about: epoxy. Although epoxy had been in use for building yachts since the early 1970s, it was still regarded with suspicion by many in the boating world, who felt it was still unproven and who thought that its famous gap-filling properties were merely a licence for shoddy workmanship. To the wooden boat purists, using epoxy was comparable to Bob Dylan taking up the electric guitar, and you could almost hear the shouts of 'Judas' as, one by one, wooden boatbuilders adopted the technique – some less reluctantly than others – and more and more epoxy ply boats were launched to a willing public.

PREVIOUS PAGE *The Acorn Skiff was one of the first boats to be designed for the new epoxy ply technique. (Photo: courtesy Iain Oughtred.)*

For Iain, the best thing about epoxy plywood construction was that you could produce strong, lightweight hulls with minimal internal framework. The epoxy seams gave the hull most of its structural rigidity, which meant that almost all the frames or ribs, apart from a couple in way of the seats, or thwarts, could be disposed of. The result was a huge saving in weight, as well as a cleanness of line which gave the hull an altogether more modern appearance.

But Iain had never built a boat this way before, and there was little published information available about the method. Mostly, he had to work things out for himself and unlearn habits ingrained from years of working with traditional glues. For a start, whereas an adhesive such as Cascamite liked nothing more than a close-fitting, tightly-clamped joint to create a good bond, epoxy by contrast worked better with a looser-fitting, more gently-clamped joint which didn't squeeze all the glue out. Later, as he experimented with filleting, the differences would become even greater.

He was, as usual, short of money and couldn't afford to pay London levels of rent. Instead, he had persuaded Nigel Irens to lend him his caravan, which he parked in a friend's garden in Cookham. It was a long cold winter, however, and he would regularly wake up with ice on the inside of the windows and come back from work to find his vegetables frozen and unmalleable. In his spare time, he had a job replacing the woodwork on a Morris Traveller using the new-fangled epoxy. With temperatures dipping as low as −15°C, however, he had to back up the car to the boatshed door and use blankets, tarpaulins and a fan heater to make sure the glue set properly. It was, he says, a 'miserable winter'.

The boat he built during those cold, lonely months, however, proved to be a turning point in his career. Soon after building the Acorn Skiff, Iain sent photos of the construction process to *WoodenBoat* magazine in America. It was, no doubt, just one submission among dozens the

BELOW *In his early 40s, Iain finally found a career he could devote himself to. (Photo: courtesy Welmoed Bouhuys.)*

magazine received every week, but it caught the eye of Maynard Bray, the technical editor, who decided to write the boat up. Although not without criticism, his review was largely enthusiastic.

'The Acorn Skiff is primarily a rowboat,' he wrote in the January/February 1984 issue of *WoodenBoat*. 'She is light in weight, narrow at the waterline, and her freeboard is kept low to keep down her windage. She rows like a dream. With her rising forefoot and lean hindquarters, she should settle back and tow well behind another boat if she were used as a tender. She'll also sail when fitted with one of the two rigs, the rudder and the dagger board shown on the drawings. But make no mistake – she is neither particularly stable nor particularly burdensome. If you're looking for a boat that you and your passengers can clomp around in, stay away from this one. She's a sweet-lined, slippery little jewel – and one in which you'll not normally want to take more than two passengers.'

But the Acorn Skiff wasn't just a pretty boat; she also represented a significant departure from the prevailing trend of the era. For the wooden boat revival in the United States was largely founded on building faithful replicas of traditional boats using traditional methods and materials. It was as much about craft as design, and there were countless 'how-to' articles in *WoodenBoat* showing how to cut a keel rebate or stem joint in the traditional manner. But there were many within the movement who felt that, if the

revival was to have a future, it couldn't simply carry on replicating the past – it had to find a new idiom for the new times. That medium, they believed, was lapstrake plywood.

'We were beginning then to realize the benefits of glued lapstrake construction and, with Joel White as designer, had helped inspire Joel's Shearwater – which was the first of Joel's designs using glued lapstrake plywood,' recalls Maynard, some 25 years after his original story was published. 'For boats of the Acorn's type, we had at the time only delineations of existing plank-on-frame craft – like, for example, those in Chapelle's *American Small Sailing Craft* and those depicted occasionally by John Gardner in *National Fisherman*. To the best of my knowledge, Iain's Acorn was the first Whitehall type of glued lap construction – and if not the first, surely the most lovely to be so built to date.'

The Acorn, then, was the right boat at the right time. The design looked familiar enough to US boaters and the construction was of the moment – plus the boat just worked well. Although the vessel's lines were changed and refined over the years, including making the stem deeper and straighter and the transom smaller and more 'Whitehall-like', the sheerline has remained unchanged from that very first drawing and, 25 years later, was described even by the usually self-deprecating Iain as a 'stroke of genius'.

As well as placing him on the map, the Acorn played another important role in Iain's nascent career: it provided him with a regular trickle of money. After the article was published, *WoodenBoat* listed the plans in their design catalogue, and there was an immediate surge of interest, with 83 plans selling in the first three months. The flow of orders gradually eased from the initial peak but it remained steady. It wasn't enough to live on yet, but it was a start.

It was around this time that Peter Spectre, *WoodenBoat*'s managing editor, visited Britain. Although Iain had by then submitted the Acorn plans to the magazine, Maynard's article had yet to be published and Peter was only vaguely aware of him. He had come to Britain not to meet Iain, or any other boatbuilder for that matter, but to research an article about mud. His office mate, Maynard Bray, had just returned from Britain and noticed that the Brits seemed to have a rather special relationship with mud – in particular mud berths and mud flats and the like – and had sent Peter to find out more.

Perhaps inevitably, he ended up at Maldon in Essex, which has a long and noble association with mud and, perhaps equally inevitably, once there he ended up at the door of university-graduate-turned-boatbuilder Fabian Bush. The events that followed were later described by Peter in an article in *WoodenBoat* and made for hilarious reading as the over-enthusiastic Fabian dragged the American reporter from one wooden boat hot spot to another. 'By early evening, I'm tired by the intensity,' Peter wrote. 'By mid-evening, I'm exhausted.'

Eventually, the pair fetched up on Osea Island, the former torpedo boat base and addiction treatment centre linked to the mainland by a tidal causeway, where Fabian was house-sitting for a friend and had a workshop in an old barn. 'We stop at a large building and go inside. The main room is dominated by a fireplace along the far wall. Seated on a bench in front of the fire, which provides the only light, is a thin bearded fellow drinking from a goblet. I can't see much of the rest of the room; if it doesn't have paintings of yachts, fowling pieces, mounted deer heads on the walls, stuffed grouse and ship models on the tabletops, it should.

'"Meet Ian Outred [sic]," says Fabian. "He designs boats."'

Iain had formed an informal partnership with Fabian after the pair met through mutual Quaker friends. Like Iain, Fabian had taken the long route to boatbuilding via a degree in social sciences, followed by two years as a bookseller and, eventually, an apprenticeship with legendary British boatbuilder Arthur Holt. When, in 1982, Iain approached him to build a Blackfish Dory for a client, Fabian took the opportunity to leave the Holt yard and set up on his own. It was the beginning of a short but productive partnership. Iain was always more of a designer than a builder, while Fabian always aspired to designing his own boats but really excelled in the minutiae of boat construction.

In his article, Peter would later compare their relationship to Phil Bolger and Harold 'Dynamite' Payson in the US – presumably with Iain as the cerebral Bolger and Fabian as the more down-to-earth Payson – before making a more musical analogy:

'Already I can sense that it's a Simon and Garfunkel deal. Fabian is the realist, the pragmatist; Iain is the idealist, the dreamer. How can I tell? Fabian wants to show me his boats. Iain wants to talk about the design process – not the hows of his boats, but the whys. Fabian talks about the endless search for ways to keep down the cost of boatbuilding and the prices of boats as means of luring customers to the door. Iain talks about craftsmanship and quality and excellence, under the assumption that these elements carpet the path to a resurgence of wooden boats in Great Britain. I can smell the fundamental agreement-to-disagree in the air.'

Whatever differences of opinion they may have had about the best way of achieving their goal, Iain and Fabian shared an all-consuming passion for wooden boats and a belief that they could stem the tide of the fibreglass invasion. And, whereas the wooden or 'classic' boat movement, in Europe at least, would become increasingly associated with expensive, highly-polished restorations and new-builds, the original motivation of these early pioneers came from far more populist, if not socialist, impulse.

'We definitely had a mission,' Fabian remembers. 'Our ethos was informed by the ideas of William Morris – the idea of producing fine-quality things for the masses. We were moving into a period of mass production, with bad craftsmanship and bad materials. We wanted to show

A clean-shaven Fabian and a bewhiskered Iain take their small boat revolution to the Southampton Boat Show, c1983. (Photo: courtesy Welmoed Bouhuys.)

that you could still hand-build wooden boats with good craftsmanship and good materials. We wanted to build beautiful boats for the masses.

'In those days, wood still had the edge over GRP in terms of performance. It was before modern materials such as epoxy and Kevlar became commonplace, and GRP construction was still quite crude. It was the days of Westerly bumbling along, going bankrupt all the time. Wood construction could still be competitive on price, especially for heavy displacement boats. There was still a hope that you could build small wooden boats and attract customers not just because they were pretty but because they represented good value for money.'

Nowadays, Iain is dismissive of the idea that they were on any kind of mission, saying that he was 'just doing what [he] had to do'. Speaking to Peter Spectre in 1985, however, he was rather more effusive. 'Why we're talking about wooden boats instead of cheap plastic boats is because of the difference in quality. Just demonstrating to people that this kind of craftsmanship is valid and useful, regardless of what it might cost, that it is something that people need to appreciate and be aware of. If you can get into that awareness, that consciousness, then that's going to affect everything they look at, everything they live with, everything they do.'

Whatever their motivation, both men needed to get the boats out there and find an audience for their ideas. Iain had had some limited success at publicizing his designs through the mainstream sailing magazines of the day, but sales of his plans were still sluggish and nowhere near enough to live on. So they decided to exhibit two boats in the dinghy park at the Southampton Boat Show, which was the best-attended venue for small boats at the time. Fabian would build an original size Acorn Skiff, while Iain would build his updated and lengthened 15ft version of the Acorn.

And so the British wooden boat revival took another significant step forward in September 1983, when Iain and Fabian took their boats to Southampton and stood outside in the wind and the rain with all the other boatbuilders and tried to sell their idea of 'beautiful boats for the masses'. They weren't the only people exhibiting wooden boats. The evergreen Jack Chippendale was there with his range of 'stitch and tape' kit boats; David Austin with his

Chippendale-designed paddling canoe; and John Kerr with a Bolger-designed skiff whose sheer, Iain decided, had 'gone funny', even though John refused to admit it.

But they were all the 'old guard' of wooden boatbuilding – the time-served, doughty upholders of a tradition that was by then all but dead. Iain and Fabian represented the 'new guard': mostly highly-educated, quasi-amateur builders who turned to boatbuilding as a lifestyle choice rather than as a necessary means to earn a crust. For, in truth, most of the professional boatbuilders had long ago realized that, if they wanted to make money, they would have to turn their hand either to fitting out fibreglass hulls or, if they were being really pragmatic, making kitchens and windows for the building trade.

The public reaction to the two Acorns on Iain's and Fabian's stand was mainly astonishment that such beautifully-crafted wooden boats were still being built. Most were appreciative of the skill that had gone into building them, although one particularly unkind visitor did suggest the trailer, with its Austin 7 wheels, might be worth more than the 'outmoded' craft sitting on it. But when it came to parting with their hard-earned cash, they stuck with their trusty fibreglass hulls. Fabian sold his boat, but Iain's went unsold, and it would be months before any of the trickle of enquiries turned into solid orders for boats. If this was the way a movement began, it was not with a bang but a stutter.

By then, Iain had moved out of his cold caravan at Cookham Dean and had found a bedsit in a stylish old house at South End Green which was more to his liking. It was a spacious room with a largish bay window with an oblique view of Hampstead Heath. There was a minimal kitchen, storage under the bed and a bare light bulb hanging from the ceiling. A plank over the steps acted as a gangway over which he could wheel his precious motorbike to protect it from the elements – an important consideration. It was hardly luxurious, but by placing his drawing board at the window, he could enjoy the view of the Heath and the activity on the street below and feel part of the living world once again.

To pay the rent, he had taken a job at a wholefood store in Hampstead run by an enthusiastic Sardinian who apparently thought nothing of picking up old vegetables that had been thrown out of the nearby Covent Garden market and selling them as 'organic' produce, at suitably inflated prices. He attended Mensa meetings ('surprisingly uninteresting'), joined the William Morris Society and went to folk clubs and music festivals. He even bought an old Hornet racing dinghy for £75 – the same boat once raced by the Hornet 'king' Beecher Moore – which he fixed up and sailed on the Thames for a few months, before deciding that he needed to sort out how he was going to feed himself first, before indulging in owning a boat.

Money was as tight as ever, but then Iain had already worked out that he wasn't going to make his fortune by building boats. 'When I was building the Acorn Skiff, this guy in Bristol lent me £1,000,' he says. 'I had made a detailed proposal about how many boats I was going to build with the money, and it looked quite impressive. There wasn't much to spare, and I would have to work hard, but as long as I sold the boats it would work out. It was all totally fanciful. I soon ran out of money and didn't have any boats to sell. Even when I did finish the first boat, I didn't immediately sell it and right away start building half a dozen more. It took about a year and a half to sell that boat for a little bit more than the cost of the materials I put into it. The second boat sold three or four years later for £1,000.'

Certainly, on the face of it, the maths didn't look good, and any businessman worth his salt would have quietly advised Iain to cash in his tools and find a proper job. But the reality

James, Fabian, Welmoed and Iain with an Acorn dinghy loaded on the car behind, in Maldon 1983. (Photo: courtesy Welmoed Bouhuys.)

was that boatbuilding was only a sideline for Iain; a useful way to test his designs and refine some of the details that he could then incorporate in his plans. The finished boats themselves were useful marketing tools too, whether being exhibited at boat shows or being featured in magazine articles. The more beautifully they were made, the more likely people were to want to build one for themselves, and the more plans Iain was likely to sell. It was a marketing strategy of sorts, although the short-term reality was that he ended up building a lot of boats for very little money.

Iain, however, was driven by something deeper than profit, a point picked up by his former business partner Fabian. 'I always regarded Iain as an artist. He was being an individualist and an enthusiast, and he wasn't interested in material wealth. He lived on no money, but he had to do that in order to focus on his work. Because, as soon as you start thinking about ways of earning money, then you get diverted from the main task. It's only by living like that, that he could achieve what he achieved.'

Peter Spectre, the American journalist who stumbled across Fabian and Iain while they were building the two Acorns which they hoped would transform the face of British boatbuilding, seems to agree with this vision of Iain (and to a lesser extent Fabian) as the starving young artist(s) in the garret. 'They were interesting characters and, to be frank, both a little crazy. Iain was broke and was living on nothing. But I was struck by the beauty of his designs. He was an artist, not just a designer, and in my view you can't be an artist unless you're a little crazy and living on the edge, and you can't be living on the edge unless you're broke.'

It was around this time too that Iain met a Dutch woman who was to play an important role in his life. Following his interest in self-development, in January 1983 Iain booked himself into an Experience Week at the Findhorn Foundation, an alternative eco-community based in north-east Scotland. There, he got talking to Welmoed Bouhuys, a primary school teacher from Holland. Welmoed (pronounced 'Velmut') remembers the meeting well. 'He was very quiet – there was nothing very outstanding about him. The first thing he said to me was, "Have you seen my boats?"

And then he showed me pictures of his designs. He was a strange bird; very softly spoken. After speaking to him for a little while, though, I realized he was a really special guy.'

So special that, two weeks after the course finished, Welmoed decided to pack up her things and move to London to work with him. She didn't know anything about boat design or boatbuilding, although she had crewed a few times on a friend's fibreglass cruiser, so she knew the rudiments of sail. But, more than that, she admired Iain and felt that even if she could only help in a simple way she would somehow be helping advance a much bigger cause. With her own children grown up and gone, she was ready for change and helping Iain was a way of giving her life extra meaning and purpose. And it certainly seemed as if he might need help.

'I went to London and saw how he lived, eating a little porridge and standing on one leg drawing. He could never be bothered with housework and cooking. As long as he had something to sit on and could keep his feet warm and had something to eat, that was enough. So I came and did some shopping and made things nice for him. He was always at his drawing board, wherever he was, he was always drawing, drawing... I've known him when he was down to his last fiver and half an apple, and he was still always drawing.'

But Welmoed didn't just help Iain with the domestic chores he found so burdensome, she also became his trainee boatbuilder and, starting with the 15ft Acorn built on Osea Island, helped him turn many designs from lines on paper into hulls on the sea. And, as she learned about boatbuilding, he was able to observe which techniques worked best for an amateur and

Welmoed puts the finishing touches to Iain's Acorn 15, while Fabian (standing) has his Acorn Skiff rigged. (Photo: courtesy Iain Oughtred.)

how best to express himself in order to describe those techniques, something that would come in useful when it came to writing more detailed building instructions later on.

It was an arrangement that would continue, on and off, for the next 15 years and which gave Welmoed a unique insight into Iain's character.

'Wherever he is, Iain is always himself. He doesn't pretend to be anything else. He can talk about many things, like music, art and literature – even when he had no money, he always found a way to buy books. But he is completely self-taught because he hated school, and he doesn't take things from other people. He'd rather work it out for himself. He doesn't like to waste time doing things he doesn't want to do, like listening to music he doesn't like or going out and making chitchat. I used to play the piano and harmonica to him sometimes, but he hated that and he didn't pretend to like it, he just told me to stop it. He's very honest like that.'

Fabian was more sanguine. 'Iain is a great artist,' he says. 'But like all great artists, they are interested in what other people are doing, but they come first. He was self-engrossed and one-track minded, but he could also be extremely generous and caring for people in trouble – once he had noticed they were in trouble.'

Perhaps inevitably, the pair's partnership was coming under strain as the roles of designer and builder became increasingly blurred. Iain was approached by a customer wanting Fabian to build Iain's latest design, but instead of passing him on to Fabian, Iain decided to build the boat himself. And, rather than building her at the workshop in Osea, he found space at an

BELOW LEFT *Welmoed and Iain pose in front of the temporary workshop at St Ives in Cambridge. (Photo: courtesy Iain Oughtred.)*

BELOW *Getting to grips with the sticky stuff, building the prototype John Dory. (Photo: courtesy Iain Oughtred.)*

alternative community at St Ives on the River Ouse near Cambridge. It was another chance to experience a different alternative community, as well as saving rent in the process – always a concern close to his heart. Once again, Welmoed came up and helped him put together the prototype of a design that would become one of the most successful in the Oughtred stable: the 18ft 3in John Dory.

Once again, Iain had turned to the dory design for its famed seakeeping properties, but this time he had homed in on the so-called Swampscott type used on the coast of Massachusetts. Built with finer ends and less overhang than the Banks dory, the Swampscott is said to be the ultimate development of the dory type. Iain adapted the design for plywood construction, adding a bit of rocker in the keel and a bulkhead fore and aft, although he nevertheless describes the John Dory design as 'pure Swampscott'.

And certainly the pictures of Welmoed rowing the newly-finished boat on the glassy waters of the Ouse look idyllic. But *Asphodel*, as the first boat was called, wasn't destined for inland waters. Her owner, a young doctor by the name of Alastair Bremner, intended her for family holidays on the Isles of Scilly, an area famed for its strong currents and choppy waters. The boat soon got her first taste of strong weather when Iain delivered her from St Mary's to St Martin's in the Scilly Isles in a Force 7 wind. He later described the experience in an article for the magazine *Chasse Marée*.

'It isn't the most sensible thing to do, to launch oneself on a new boat across such treacherous and unknown waters, with ugly-looking rocks standing between us and any sign of land. But *Asphodel* seems so confident, so impatient to get sailing, that we can't bear to disappoint her, and so we set off out to sea, surfing the waves in grand style. The boat is manageable and forgiving but requires concentration, and we are happy to arrive at our destination.'

The following day, the pair went out again, this time in a Force 6 with triple-reefed main. As the boat was buffeted by sudden gusts, Iain reflected that it might be a good idea to fit a smaller sail to make the ride a bit more 'relaxed', but concluded that 'it's hard to imagine what sea could put [the boat] in difficulty'. The accompanying picture, showing a delighted Iain at the helm, proved the point.

Meanwhile, Fabian had been busy designing and building his own version of an American dory, although, as this one was intended to be rowed across the Atlantic, it had little of the finesse of Iain's design (the boat, called *In Finnegans Wake*, did nevertheless carry Michael Nestor and Sean Crowley safely from the Canary Islands to the West Indies in a time of 73 days in January–April 1986). And then there was his Blackwater Sailing Canoe, a half-decked camper-cruiser described by one writer as 'the best hope for British wooden boat building', to add to his own growing list of designs. He had also built a curious 21ft steam boat designed by Iain and based on, of all things, the lines of a Swampscott dory.

'After exhibiting at Southampton, we got orders for several boats, but there was a bit of conflict over who should design what,' says Fabian. 'I had designed the Atlantic dory, which he didn't like. With Iain, it was all about aesthetics, whereas I tried to mix form and function more. I had the, probably erroneous, idea that you could make boats more economical by designing them more simply. Phil Bolger showed how that could be done. For instance, when I was building a boat I would fit a rubbing strake, with a layer of spruce on the inside and a layer of teak on the outside, all glued and screwed together. Bolger just did away with the rubbing strake altogether – which saved a lot of work!'

With so much activity from his two 'crazy' boatbuilder friends, no wonder Peter Spectre found reason for optimism when he returned to England in March 1985. He wrote up the story of both meetings in the May/June 1986 issue of *WoodenBoat* under the headline 'In Search of the British Wooden Boat Revival – On the Waterfront with Iain and Fabian'. It was a well-timed piece of journalism designed to spur the well-meaning but largely apathetic revivalists into action. It ended with this provocative statement: 'Some of the boatbuilders in Britain are despondent, many are not, but overall one's impression is that the British wooden boat building scene is down but not out, waiting for a catalyst that will kick it forward after years of being presumed to be dead.'

Speaking 22 years later, he says, 'We knew there was something going on in Britain, but no one was reporting on it. I went to see Peter Freebody [one of the top boat restorers and builders on the Thames] and asked him what else had been written about him, and he showed me one small article written by a German magazine, and that was it.'

Even before Peter's article was published, there were developments on the ground which suggested that the long-awaited British revival might finally be on its way. In the spring of 1985, Iain received a new commission – this time not for a boat but for a book. Jane Weeks at Nautical Books (later press officer at the National Maritime Museum) had come to the conclusion that there were many more wooden boatbuilders and designers scattered about the country than people realized. What was needed was a directory to showcase their work and make them more visible to the general boating public and Iain, she decided, was the man to put it together.

Wooden Boatbuilding in Britain – A Guide to Designers, Builders & Suppliers, published in January 1986, was a daring undertaking considering the degree of pessimism surrounding the subject at that time. Unlike Paul Lipke's *Plank on Frame*, published five years earlier during the first flush of the American wooden boat revival, its British equivalent virtually anticipates

Asphodel *is put through her paces sailing among the Scilly Isles. Owner Alastair Bremmer is amidships. (Photo: Donald Bremner.)*

Iain in positive mode at Hampstead in 1985, about to start work on his directory of wooden boatbuilders. (Photo: courtesy Welmoed Bouhuys.)

the movement that it attempts to describe. It took Iain five weeks to mail out questionnaires to over 500 builders and designers and collate all their responses. Initially intended as a paperback, the book grew to a 194-page hardback by the time he finished, with the details of over 200 boatbuilders and designers contained within it. The feedback was surprisingly upbeat. At least 75% of boatbuilders contacted felt the market was improving (though, arguably, it could hardly have got worse), 69% had a building or restoration job in progress and 59% had at least one job lined up for the future.

Not surprisingly, several of Iain's designs featured in the book, including the sail plan of the Acorn 15 and a preliminary sketch of a 19ft canoe yawl. There are also photos of the Blackfish Dory (wrongly described in the caption, ironically enough, as the Acorn 15) and the steam canoe built by Fabian. Iain is listed twice in the directory, both as designer and builder, although, with typical modesty, both his entries are about half as long as everyone else's. The entries themselves, written by the aspiring designer just as he was starting to make a name for himself, shed interesting light on how he perceived himself and his future career. In the design section, he writes:

'Specializing in traditionally-inspired designs, for present-day use and construction methods. I aim for performance, but not at the expense of enjoying oneself. I am impressed by US tradition and development, but feel the need to give expression to British roots and inspiration. I am working on a range of clinker plywood dinghies and skiffs, and dories, and plan to do some sailing canoes, and simple dinghy cruisers; at present I am working on a proposal for a light, fast 40ft home-buildable cruiser.'

Ever the dreamer, in the boatbuilding section, he describes his future expectations as: 'Ideally a small shop in a beautiful setting on the water, where interesting boats can be built when the opportunity comes up, and prototypes of new designs, and perhaps stock traditional style dinghies and kit boats for "bread & butter".' Hardly the words of a committed boatbuilder hustling for business, but by then Iain's destiny was already carved out elsewhere. Curiously, his ideal of 'a small shop in a beautiful setting on the water' was soon to be realized – albeit not in the way he probably imagined. Fabian, incidentally, didn't warrant a listing in the designers section, although he is given generous coverage in the boatbuilders listing and shown sailing his immaculate Osea Brig, which he designed and built himself. In his entry, he claims to build nearly four boats a year, compared to Iain's one.

The book also reveals Iain's own growing bias against epoxy and contains a heart-felt comment about using the adhesive in colder climes – no doubt harking back to his own 'miserable winter' at Cookham Dean. 'Epoxy has not transformed wooden boatbuilding, as some seem to believe, but it makes possible some new techniques such as "filleting", by which, for example, a bulkhead may be joined to the hull side without the need for any framing. A real problem in cold weather has been the necessity to warm the glue and wood to a certain temperature – the makers appear to assume that all boat shops are equipped with central heating – but there is now one type available which sets in cold weather.'

Elsewhere, however, he concedes that epoxy has made clinker plywood 'more feasible' for amateurs because of its gap-filling properties, and he goes on to describe epoxy-ply as 'a very

light and strong construction, with a lot of the attractiveness of traditional timber'. These contradictory signals suggest the beginnings of a disenchantment with – or at least an ambivalence towards – a construction method that would increasingly dominate wooden boatbuilding and in whose success he would, ironically, play a significant part.

At the time the book was written, however, a revival of any sorts was still looking shaky, and in his Introduction Iain bemoaned the lack of a 'rallying point'. He pointed out that, whereas *WoodenBoat* had achieved an 'almost mythical' status, there was no such equivalent in Britain. The result was that many British boatbuilders read *WoodenBoat* and were consequently influenced by its philosophies and designs, rather than looking towards Britain's own rich boating heritage. Already then, he was thinking more deeply about the significance of small boat designs beyond the mere fact that they were made of wood.

Iain's appeal seemed to have the desired effect and, within a year of the book's publication, several 'rallying points' started to spring up. First off was a magazine called *Classic Boat*, launched in 1987, which, although not devoted exclusively to wooden boats, would champion the cause of traditional craft in Britain and further afield. The same year, the first Greenwich Wooden Boat Show was organized on the lawns of the National Maritime Museum as a celebration of small, traditional craft. The first event was a washout and few exhibitors turned up, but it sowed the seed for a bigger turnout the following year and, for a while at least, the show would become the meeting point for the movement. Elsewhere in 1986, a classic yacht regatta was initiated at Shotley Point Marina in Suffolk, followed a year later by a similar event in Falmouth, Cornwall. At last, it seemed, the British wooden boat revival was more than just wishful thinking among a handful of diehard traditionalists: it was a live and happening phenomenon.

Just as things were getting interesting in Britain, however, Iain received an invitation he couldn't refuse. And, this time, it didn't have an Australian stamp on it.

IAIN ON *ASPHODEL*

(Extract from building notes)

The John Dory *Asphodel* was built in Cambridgeshire in the spring of 1984. Her owner spends his summers in the Scilly Isles, 28 miles off Land's End, out in the Atlantic Ocean. Warmed by the Gulf Stream, the islands have a more temperate climate than the rest of Britain, with much exotic vegetation. The water is clear and blue; the beaches have fine white sand. The pale-skinned English people who holiday there have the feeling they are somewhere else, a lot further south. However, some rugged weather comes in from the west; the sailing waters and beaches are quite exposed. So a very seaworthy and manageable boat was required; one that would perform well under oars or sail, and be light enough to haul up the beach. […]

Asphodel's owner wanted a large sail area, so the original rig was increased to 90 square feet. A short mast was reckoned to be essential for heavy weather, and because she would be on a fairly exposed mooring for three months of the year. The standing lug rig was fitted with a sprit boom. […]

Asphodel was launched with due ceremony on the river, near Cambridge. Among the ducks and lily pads and willow trees, under the medieval bridge she seemed, as she was, a long way from the Atlantic Ocean. But she rested lightly on the water, with a kind of grace and self-assurance. It intrigues me, how boats change when they meet the water … all these months she has been a construction in the shop, and now suddenly she becomes something different – she comes to life. She seemed to be saying: All right, here I am; what would you like me to do for you – I'm ready.

She rowed fast, as expected. Many friends had come for her big day, so we had the chance to try her with many combinations of crew weight. Two or three seemed ideal; she would glide along effortlessly and silent, and would just keep on going when the oars were shipped. The wake of passing powerboats she would treat with disdain, gently rising and falling, as dories seem to do, instead of the expected roll and lurch. The buoyancy increases rapidly as the hull is immersed, due to the flare of the sides: four kids added to the three adults hardly seemed to affect her. With this weight, she still had freeboard to spare in sheltered water; loaded thus she is very steady in the water.

Single-handed, the forefoot is only just immersed. She has more rocker in the bottom than traditional dories; another advantage of plywood planking. (Heavy fore-and-aft planks being harder to fit, where the fine pointed ends meet the chines.) *Asphodel* also has no skeg; these two factors mean that she is rather wayward when lightly laden. Which is great for manoeuvrability: she can turn in her own length if not going fast. But I found it required a little too much concentration to keep her moving in a straight line, especially if the breeze was a bit gusty. […]

Asphodel was trailed to Penzance, in Cornwall. She would happily have sailed across to Scilly, but it would have meant a longish wait for the weather, so we put her on the ferry for St Mary's, leaving an early 5 mile sail to St Martin's. As we rigged her on the beach, the locals were shaking their heads, saying it was blowing Force 8 outside – that's 35 to 40 knots – and generally expressing scepticism about our chances of survival. Especially as we had a bit of gear to carry, and a 6ft dinghy to her tender – to be towed across. So we tucked in a second reef and decided to give her a tentative ride across the harbour and back before heading out. The dinghy was obviously holding her back, but she felt easy enough, so we had a look at the open water, and it looked to be blowing about a Force 6, around 25 knots, which seemed feasible as it was a run down to St Martin's. But with a new boat, strange and rough waters, with spiky looking rocks between us and any visible land … But *Asphodel* seemed so confident, so impatient to get on with it, that we felt we could not disappoint her, and so pointed her downhill – and away she went, surfing down the seas in great style. She felt very buoyant and manageable, though demanding concentration owing to the drag of the dinghy and the course, which was about as close to a dead run as I felt comfortable with.

The following day we got around 30 knots of wind

out of the west. With three reefs, leaving her with only about 45 square foot of sail, and without the dinghy she really came to life. We didn't expect to make dramatic progress to windward against this much wind and sea, with so little sail; but she forged ahead in a very determined manner, nicely under control, really making ground and a lot drier than I expected to be in such conditions. We could sit up on the gunwale for a bit more power, but it felt a bit precarious without toestraps, and made no noticeable difference to the speed. It seemed that an even smaller sail would be enough in a stronger breeze, and would still get her to windward, with a more relaxed ride downwind. [...]

Another surprise with the dory comes when bearing away to a reach: she does not go any faster! Well, hardly – the easily driven hull reaches its maximum speed quite quickly, getting very close to it in sheltered water on the wind. But, not being a planing shape, she will not get up and go like a dinghy as the sheets are eased. This makes little difference when it is light; in fact in drifting conditions she slides along remarkably quickly, due to the low wetted surface.

Downwind in the breeze she surfed fast down the waves, rolling around a bit, but always directionally steady and controllable. She seems to have no inclination to broach, and gybing is extraordinarily

easy. It isn't easy to imagine a sea that would get her into trouble in normal conditions; perhaps ultimately a big breaking crest could swamp the boat. The unstayed rig means that the sail can be let fly, forward of the mast, or instantly dropped if necessary. [...]

Alastair did not give the impression of being a fanatical racing sailor, but *Asphodel* seems to have aroused his competitive instinct, and he sends glowing accounts of his latest victories. These include: Drascombe 21; a local Banks dory; a 19ft Cornish Coble; even a Mirror 16. He overheard some guys in St Mary's on the quay, asking each other what kind of a boat it was: 'I'm sure I don't know', said one, 'but she goes like s**t off a shovel'.

This is not what she's for, either, in fact. But I guess I am inclined to be aware of performance potential in all details of a design, even if speed is not the primary purpose of the boat. It's part of the challenge in fact, to get as much of it as possible without compromising the design in other ways; I don't at all mind going fast in any kind of boat if it can be achieved without hard work, discomfort or danger. The ability of this dory to get to windward in a strong wind would be very comforting if one were setting off on a cruise in unsettled weather.

chapter 4
AMONG FRIENDS IN MAINE

WITH ITS VAST TRACTS of unspoilt forests and miles of virgin coastline, Maine had long been a focus for America's 'back to the earth' movement. Traditional skills such as organic farming, carpentry and weaving had been revived as a reaction against the mass-production approach which dominated mainstream society. Traditional boatbuilding fitted in perfectly with this ethos, and Maine soon became the centre of the wooden boat revival not just for the USA but for most of the world.

In 1974, into this fertile environment, former boatbuilder Jon Wilson launched what was to become the voice of the movement: *WoodenBoat* magazine. Aimed at the amateur and professional boatbuilder, it was packed to the gills with practical and historical articles about (mostly) indigenous American craft. Within a year the magazine had attracted 8,000 subscribers, and by the end of its third year it employed a staff of twelve and its circulation had risen to 25,000. By 1981 it was secure enough to move to grandiose new offices in Brooklin on a 60-acre estate overlooking Eggemoggin Reach, on the east side of Penobscot Bay. There, with the participation of eminent figures such as yacht designer Joel White and authors Maynard Bray and Peter Spectre, the magazine continued to expand and set up its own programme of boatbuilding and sailing courses. By the mid-1980s its circulation was over 100,000, where it has remained ever since. Clearly, as Wilson wrote in his very first editorial, it was a magazine 'whose time has come'.

One of the publication's early followers was a racing boat nut on the other side of the Pacific. 'Iain first came to my attention when *WoodenBoat* magazine was still operating out of my living room, back in the woods of coastal Maine,' remembers Jon Wilson. 'I can vividly recall the artistic script of his letters, always accented by the small pen-and-ink sketches of what I took to be the boats of his dream life. He was in Australia then, as I remember, and he was clearly passionate about the future for traditional wooden boats. Iain is one of a handful of early correspondents whose work and words I recall this well.'

By the early-1980s, when Iain was building his Acorn Skiff, the American wooden boat revival was going great guns and there was clear frustration at the *WoodenBoat* offices that the movement had failed to spread to the other side of the Atlantic to the same extent. It must therefore have come as something of a shock when, out of the blue, Iain sent in a set of drawings and photos of his clinker plywood dinghy built on the banks of the River Thames. For the

Since 1981 WoodenBoat has been based in the idyllic setting of a 60-acre estate on Eggemoggin Reach, Maine. (Photo: Kip Brundage.)

Acorn Skiff was not only a particularly accomplished interpretation of a quintessential American craft; its modern clinker plywood construction meant that it was in many ways more advanced than anything coming out of America.

As Maynard Bray explains, the decision to invite Iain for a three-month sabbatical in Maine, for which the magazine would provide flights, board and lodging, was not entirely selfless. 'We thought Iain's Acorn showed him to have an unusually fine eye for form and beauty and, further, considered that having a designer emerge who, like our friend and colleague Joel, could also build what he drew, was something we wanted to support. So *WoodenBoat* invited Iain to come to Brooklin so that, together, we could all push forward on the glued lapstrake frontier. Exposure of that kind would benefit all, we thought. And so it did.'

Iain's acceptance into the *WoodenBoat* fold came at a timely point in his career. The magazine was already selling plans for five of his designs – indeed the Acorn Skiff was their second best-seller, after Joel White's Nutshell pram – but he was still not designing full time and it would be a long time before he would describe himself as a 'professional' boat designer. Life in London suited him better than life in Sydney, but he was still socially isolated and knew few people with whom he could share his passion for sailing and boatbuilding. Little wonder that he jumped at the chance to leave his draughty bedsit in Hampstead to spend a few months at the epicentre of the wooden boat world.

Iain arrived in Brooklin in July 1986 and was given a room above the boatbuilding school, appropriately enough, in the grounds of the *WoodenBoat* estate. He had no fixed job, no fixed hours and no fixed location; his only task was to observe and contribute as seemed appropriate. Inevitably, he spent a great deal of time in the boatbuilding school, where Jim Brown and John Marples (both designers in their own right) oversaw the construction of various canoes and dinghies. Iain watched dozens of Nutshell prams being built, and began forming his own ideas both about the design and the form of construction, which would be realized in years to come.

'Clinker plywood construction was just getting established, and the techniques were not very well researched,' says Iain. 'The Nutshell pram for instance was still being built using screws, and they had not yet tried different clamping methods. The more I looked at it, the more I thought I could improve on it.'

All in all, it was a stimulating environment which forced him to stretch out beyond his usual comfort zone. He ventured tentatively into the realm of public speaking when he gave a seminar about boat design to a group of wooden boat aficionados. He revived his old model-making skills when he helped rig a model of a Friendship sloop which *WoodenBoat* was marketing. And he practised his writing skills when he wrote a series of six articles about rigs, which were published in *WoodenBoat* magazine in subsequent months (and for which he was paid separately). It was the first time he had written about a subject he didn't already know intimately, and the first time he felt the full brunt of the editor's pen.

'There was so much material available in the library, I could research any type of sailing rig and make it sound like I knew what I was talking about – which I didn't at all. I was a little dismayed when, after I'd worked and worked to get it as good as I could, I handed it in to the editors and they tore it to bits, chopping things out and swapping paragraphs around. But then I looked closely at what they'd done, and I realized they had made it better. I realized that a good editor can see the whole story, which I can't do, because I can see only one paragraph at a time. It's like being able to look at the plans of a boat, and being able to visualize how it will look in three dimensions.'

Apart from Iain's informal duties assisting at the school and writing articles, he was assigned one major project while he was at *WoodenBoat*: to design a compact trailerable cruising boat, suitable for amateur construction. At the time, all the plans sold through the magazine's catalogue were for smaller boats, and they were keen to expand the range. There was no deadline, and Iain was to retain all the rights to the design, for which *WoodenBoat* would simply charge their usual commission for any plans they sold.

In consultation with the magazine's 'inner circle' (mainly Jon Wilson, Maynard Bray and Peter Spectre) Iain started working up some ideas and became increasingly drawn to a Scandinavian style, no doubt inspired by his visit to the Baltic all those years before. The 22ft Grey Seal (or Gray Seal, as the Americans would have it) was at the limit of what might be considered trailerable, with a displacement of 3,800lb, and was one of the biggest boats designed specifically for clinker plywood construction at that time. Even with her centreboard up, she drew 2ft 3in, while with the board down her draught was 4ft 4in. Iain later drew a deep-keel version with a 3ft 5in draught, which abandoned the pretence of being trailerable and performed just as well as her shallower sister.

It wasn't all work... Iain dancing with a woman on stilts at a craft fair in Maine. (Photo: courtesy Welmoed Bouhuys.)

Reviewing the design in *WoodenBoat* in May/June 1990, Mike O'Brien commented: 'Gray Seal represents a subtle, and we think successful, blend of Scandinavian characteristics. The designer sees this boat not as a miniature of a larger yacht, but rather as "what a faering builder might do if he wanted cruising accommodations". At any rate, the little cruiser shows a strong sheer and buoyant hull. She'll not be overwhelmed easily.'

The boat's plans were completed in 1988 and have been included in the *WoodenBoat* catalogue ever since, with well over 100 plans sold and boats being built as far afield as Finland, Japan and Australia.

Iain's time in Maine was also a sociable one, and he soon became integrated into the wooden boat scene – for the first time in his life he was surrounded by people who thought and spoke like him. In this way, Iain experienced an idealized America. It was an America where he was welcomed into people's homes, where many of those homes were made of wood and where he never had to lock up his car. It was an America where he was liked and respected in equal measure.

There were long sessions in the kitchen at the *WoodenBoat* offices, discussing the finer points of wooden boat construction. And there were evenings socializing, although as most of the staff only worked four days a week and commuted long distances to get to Brooklin, the site was often deserted from Friday to

Sunday, leaving Iain to look after himself. No doubt his hosts still regarded him as 'a little crazy', but then everyone else there was 'a little crazy' too, so it didn't much matter.

Anglophile journalist Peter Spectre was one who took the Anglo-Australian designer under his wing. 'He came to my house for Thanksgiving dinner, which was quite a way from Brooklin,' he remembers. 'He was as skinny as I've ever seen him, and he probably wasn't cooking for himself much. I've never seen a skinny guy eat so much in my life!'

With a large array of boats on hand, ranging from peapods to dories, Iain was able to test out a variety of designs and learn from their performance – something he would put to good use when designing his own boats in future years. He was particularly taken by a 10 Square Metre Canoe – said to be the last canoe built by Uffa Fox and then owned by John Hanson, publisher of *Maine Boats, Homes and Harbors* magazine, which he took on long jaunts to the islands around Eggemoggin Reach. With winter approaching and the temperature of the water plummeting, it was a feat of daring which drew admiration, and a little anxiety, from his hosts.

'I remember him sailing John Hanson's decked canoe in a brisk late November wind, fully in control and having the time of his life,' says Maynard. 'I stood onshore, worried at first, because all the other boats had been hauled for the winter and there'd be no chance of a rescue if he capsized. But then I realized Iain was completely at home in this high performance craft with its hiking board and big rig.'

Three months melted away, but so mutually beneficial was the visit that Iain's sabbatical was extended by another three months. The ever-faithful Welmoed visited in September and stayed in a nearby caravan with 'mice happily hopping around'. She even got a job helping out at *WoodenBoat*, for which she was duly paid. She too has idyllic memories of her time in Maine. 'Every Friday we had lobster on the beach, with corn on the cob. Poor lobsters, thrown into the boiling water, heated in oil drums, turning red with rage. Little do they know how tasty they are. The sailing was good there, but the water bitterly cold. I tried it once, and it was even colder than the Blackwater River in March. No way Iain would dip even a toe in. Luckily he's a master in not-capsizing!'

By now autumn was giving way to winter and, despite his prior training living in his cold caravan by the Thames, Iain struggled to come to terms with temperatures that shot way below zero. The only source of heat in his room was a woodburning stove, and he quickly had to teach himself how to use a chainsaw in order to keep the stove fed with logs. At the end of the six months his visa expired, and he had no choice but to return home to England. Although he had only partly completed one design in that period (the Grey Seal) it had nevertheless been a very productive time that would influence his thinking for years to come. He had, as he put it, learnt more in six months than he would have learnt in six years working on his own. He had also made friendships that would remain with him for the rest of his life.

The crew at *WoodenBoat*, too, had benefited not only from Iain's expertise but also gained a valued friend, as Jon Wilson suggests: 'When Iain came to live and work in our part of Maine during the early 1980s, it was wonderful to have him here. Everyone in our community loved his quiet demeanor and the simultaneously lovely and rigorous thinking of his design work, and I think it was an extremely fertile time in the evolution of his lapstrake plywood creations. I don't know if what was going on in Brooklin advanced his inventiveness in that direction, since he was already deeply immersed in the exploration, but I hope so. It was wonderful to have him living among us, and we all still miss him.'

Iain made the most of the WoodenBoat *dinghy collection, including this Uffa Fox 10 Square Metre Canoe. (Photo: courtesy Maynard Bray.)*

IAIN ON THE LUG RIG

(Extract from *WoodenBoat* November/December 1986.) (Photo: courtesy Donald Bremner.)

The standing lugsail is a wonderfully simple rig to set up and handle. The spars, rigging and fittings are about as basic as they can be, the sail can be set in a few moments and is more easily reefed than most other sails, and the spars are short enough to be stowed inside a small boat. The standing lug rig is – or can be – more elegant looking (at least in my opinion) than the spritsail because of its higher peak, and it's a more efficient windward sail (I think), less disturbed by the spars on the 'wrong' side. Brailing is less effective, perhaps, than with a spritsail, although it can be done. The yard and sail of the standing lug are more easily detached from the mast and laid in the boat. The lug has at least as much drive as a gaff sail of the same area, at least in smaller sizes, and operates with much simpler gear.

For the standing lugsail to set well, the point at which the halyard attaches to the yard is critical. Generally it is worked out by trial and error, since the ideal position varies a bit according to the shape and cut of the sail. It needs to be far enough forward to give good tension on the luff, but if it is too far ahead it allows the outer end of the yard to swing down and flail around when the sail is being raised or lowered, unless some tension is kept on the luff. At least one third back on the yard seems about right; if it gets closer to halfway, the leverage necessary for luff tension is insufficient.

On small boats, the halyard is often bent onto the yard with a clove hitch or rolling hitch, or it can be made fast with a hook to a grommet around the yard, positioned with a thumb cleat or eye. The halyard can be easily cast off from the yard this way, so the yard and sail can be separated from the mast and laid in the boat. A parrel is useful in keeping the yard close to the mast, but there are other methods, such as leading the halyard through a thimble seized to the yard, across the mast, and then to the heel of the yard. The yard should not be peaked up too high in a lugsail without a boom; a 'squarer' shape spreads the sail better downwind.

In some small boats, the yard of a standing lugsail can be dipped on tacking, but it's not always done.

Certainly it looks better not to have the sail lying on the 'wrong' side of the mast, but the difference in performance seems to be imperceptible. I find it slightly disconcerting that on opposite tacks the sail does not luff in quite the same way when sailing to windward, making it a bit hard to judge the exact angle of the apparent wind. Maybe I just need more practice, but in any case, a boat rigged this way is not in any sense a racer and a degree or two up- or downwind makes little difference.

If the yard is not to be dipped, the halyard sheave – usually a dumb sheave (an elongated hole through the mast) on small boats – may be set at an angle of about 45° to the boat's centreline. But if the yard is to be dipped, the halyard should lead fore and aft. Dipping is achieved by means of a light line attached to the heel of the yard, led aft and down around the foot of the sail, or through an eye on the boom where it can be easily reached. […]

In our evolutionary chain, the balanced lug rig is a simple and logical development of the boomed standing lug. The boom and tack are simply brought forward to overlap the mast by up to $\frac{1}{7}$ of the length of the foot. This changes the behaviour of the sail considerably when the sheet is eased in that as the boom tries to lift, it is prevented from doing so by the tension on the luff. Thus, when running in a fresh breeze, the twist in the sail is very much reduced: the foot is not sheeted in too hard and the head is not falling away – a condition that encourages rolling and the risk of an accidental gybe, and can make a small boat practically uncontrollable in a strong breeze. 'Overlapping' the boom and sail keeps the rig more rigid, making it more manageable as well as more effective for downwind work.

The balanced lugsail cannot be dipped, so on one tack it will lie entirely to windward of the mast. Its shape isn't distorted much in spite of this, because of the boom and the short distance the luff overlaps the mast. If the boom is long, however, it can cause problems because it's likely to hit the water when eased

in a gust, and if the sheet is eased further no more wind can be spilled from the sail. This limitation encourages the skipper not to press his boat too hard when sailing on the wind and seems a small price to pay in return for power and control off the wind. However, it is possible to shift the boom forward when the sail is reefed, so that the excess length projects forward, rather than aft beyond the clew. The working boatman's dislike of a boom (which he considered quite nonessential) kept the balanced lug from ever being the rig of choice in fishing and beach boats; it was used almost exclusively in recreational craft, reputedly starting on the River Thames, and became popular in several kinds of small boats.

The light sailing canoes and canoe yawls of the 1890s took the balanced lug rig a step further with the use of 'reefing battens'. The small canoes used a complex system of small blocks fastened to these battens, enabling the sail to be reefed simply by easing the halyard and hauling on one line. Larger boats used lazyjacks to aid reefing, so the sail could be lowered as far as the required reef and points tied in when it was convenient.

All of these developments led to a rig that provided good driving power on short spars and a sail plan that could be reduced quickly – a quality that's essential in light craft with very little stability.

chapter 5

A HIGHLAND FLING

AFTER ALL THE STIMULATION of working (and playing) at *WoodenBoat* for six months, coming back to England was, predictably, something of a let-down. The British wooden boat movement was showing the first signs of finally coming out of its long hibernation, with the launch of *Classic Boat* magazine, the creation of the Wooden Boat Show at the National Maritime Museum in Greenwich and a number of traditional boat regattas popping up all over the country. But, compared to the momentum Iain had experienced at the very heart of the revival in Maine, it was still scattered and sporadic.

'I never imagined a revival would be possible in Britain on the same scale or with the same variety of boats as the US. That's partly because the population is so much smaller, so it was bound to be a smaller scene, but also because the Americans have a different attitude. If they have an interesting idea about building a boat or something, they'll say, "Let's do it," and they'll do it. Whereas in Britain, we'll say, "Hmmm, that's an interesting idea. I really wish I could do that, but I don't think I can manage that right now. Maybe next year." And we'll never do it! In America, there's just more space, more freedom, more money and more opportunities.'

There was disappointment on the professional front as well. After the success of his sailing rigs series in *WoodenBoat*, Iain had thought he might be able to supplement his income by writing articles for magazines, but away from the creative buzz (and extensive library resources) of the Maine bubble, he struggled to write anything. Eventually, he put together an article on rigging small boats, which *WoodenBoat* rejected and he ended up selling to a British magazine 'for about a quarter of the price'.

Not surprisingly, one of the first designs Iain drew when he got back to Britain was inspired by his visit to the US. One of the most popular boats to be built at the *WoodenBoat* boatbuilding school was the Nutshell pram, designed by Joel White. This pretty 7ft 7in dinghy, with its transom bow, is one of the easiest projects for a beginner to tackle. It's also a versatile little boat that can be used as a training boat for kids and adults alike, or as a tender. As a result, there are usually dozens of them knocking about the *WoodenBoat* estate, either emerging from the boatbuilding shop or tacking in and out of the sailing school.

Iain had always wanted to draw a pram dinghy, and he knew it would make a good addition to his design catalogue, but the Nutshell clearly did everything it was supposed to and seemed

OPPOSITE *The Caledonia Yawl design, such as this 2003 Blekinge Archipelago Raid winner* Gjoa, *was inspired by Shetland working boats. (Photo: Nic Compton.)*

Iain's love affair with motorbikes was still going strong in 1988, when this picture was taken. (Photo: Andrew Carnegie.)

like a hard act to beat. Faced with an existing concept that already does the job very well, it's hard to see what a designer can do other than risk replicating it. But Iain wasn't so easily defeated. 'As I looked at the boat, I gradually came to the idea that I could do something,' he says. 'I could simplify the structure, so that it wouldn't have a laminated stem and frame. Laminating wood is a bit fussy for a simple pram, and it could be avoided if I just carried the flat bottom through to the bow. And I was sure I could improve the sailing rig. The Nutshell has a standing lug with a lifting boom, which is liable to twist and can be dangerous going downwind in a stiff breeze.'

The result was the Mouse pram, a 7ft 9in dinghy which, to the untrained eye, looks similar to the Nutshell (there is, after all, only so much you can do with the classic pram dinghy shape) but is slightly narrower (better for rowing), has slightly more sail area and, according to the specifications, is nearly 10lb lighter. But perhaps the biggest departure was to abandon the lug rig in favour of a smart-looking gunter rig, which effectively acts as a bermudan sail with the mast in two parts for ease of stowing. It's certainly a better-looking boat all round, though quite how Iain has managed it is hard to pin down.

After a few months back in London, Iain decided it was time to escape. His friend Eva's parents had a wonderful old house in Cobh, near Cork, and Iain was able to rent a room from them, overlooking the harbour. It was a short-term fix for the much longer-term problem of where to live, but it provided Iain with a useful breathing space as well as a chance to check out his family's Irish roots. He had by now accumulated quite a pile of possessions, including a decrepit VW Karman Ghia sportscar called Ludwig, a 1973 BMW motorbike called Biggles and a variety of interesting woodworking tools. So, in June 1987, with the help of Welmoed, a trailer and not a little shuttling between London and Swansea, he loaded most of his worldly possessions on a ferry to the Emerald Isle.

Eva's parents' house had once been a grand stately home, with outbuildings and gardens, but the facilities were basic, and the occupants were kept busy feeding fires to keep the place warm. Welmoed joined Iain towards the end of his time there, and she spent much of her time on the beach foraging to find driftwood for the woodburning stove and seaweed for the soup, as well as hanging blankets on the doors to keep the draughts out, while Iain worked on his next strand of designs.

One of the consistent threads to emerge from Iain's research for *Wooden Boatbuilding in Britain* was the predominance of American designs in preference to indigenous boats. This despite the country's wealth of traditional local craft, ranging from the cobles of Yorkshire to the prawners of Morecambe Bay, not to mention the curraghs and hookers of Ireland, and literally hundreds of other strange and wonderful vessels which had evolved all over the country to fulfil specific tasks in specific locales. Most efforts to record these boats had been consigned to museum researchers and a few enlightened writers, such as Basil Greenhill, Edgar March and Eric McKee. These writers however were mainly concerned with larger craft, such as the West Country schooners and East Coast trawlers.

By contrast, there was much more information available on American small boat designs, thanks to the effort of such luminaries as John Gardner, Phil Bolger and R D Culler – not to mention *WoodenBoat* magazine itself, founded back in 1974 and a treasure trove of articles on American craft and how to build them. If you wanted to make a wooden dinghy in the mid-1980s, it was quite simply easier to opt for a tried and tested American design than an obscure British design that no one had attempted to build for at least a generation.

Iain was no exception. Most of his early designs had taken their inspiration from the other side of the Atlantic, be it the hardy dory, the elegant Whitehall or Joel White's ubiquitous Nutshell. His own entry in *Wooden Boatbuilding in Britain*, however, showed that it was an issue that was beginning to increasingly concern him. 'I am impressed by US tradition and development,' he wrote, 'but feel the need to give expression to British roots and inspiration.'

It may have been the memories of the Scandinavian double-enders he had seen during his travels in Sweden and Norway that were reawakened while he was working on the lines of the Folkboat-inspired Grey Seal. Or it may have been that after six months of immersing himself in American designs, he was ready to tackle something with a distinctly European flavour. In any case, it wasn't long after his return to Britain that Iain got a chance to put his words into action.

The stimulus this time was a commission from an American client for a biggish dayboat, something a bit more comfortable and less performance-orientated than his other sailing dinghies, such as the Fulmar, and which could be rowed when necessary. The order came a few weeks before Iain headed off to Ireland, and he started drawing the boat at his ramshackle pad in Hackney. The idea was to base the design on the seaworthy double-ended working boats of the Shetland Islands, themselves closely related to the Scandinavian faering type. As usual, he conducted detailed research, seeking out whatever drawings of the type he could find – which in this case was very few. His academic research was fleshed out by the sight of a Peapod-style training boat moored up in Cork harbour, and by the plywood dinghies built by Rankin Boats, which proliferated in the area.

'I had no intention of trying to design an actual Shetland Yoal. The commission was for a glued plywood boat, with a completely different purpose to the original. It had to be lighter, more versatile and with better all-round sailing performance – and simple to build. At the same time, I wanted to retain the graceful character and extraordinary seagoing ability of the traditional boats.'

What Iain drew was a rugged 19ft 6in 'beachboat' which, above the water at least, bore a strong likeness to its original muse – albeit reduced from traditional clinker to a simple four-plank-a-side clinker plywood construction. Below the waterline the changes were more evident. While the old sixareens (six-oared clinker workboats from the Shetland Islands) were built with a distinct tuck in the garboard to give the hull more lateral resistance, Iain could do away with that and rely on the centreboard to stop the boat sliding to leeward under sail. This greatly reduced the need to bend planks into awkward shapes and simplified the entire building process – which was very much a part of the objective.

The design was simplified in other subtle ways too, such as doing away with the traditional 'stammeron' (stem knee) frame at either end of the boat and replacing them with conventional

TOP *A Mk III Caledonia Yawl under construction, with seven strakes per side rather than the original four. (Photo: courtesy Iain Oughtred.)*

BOTTOM LEFT *Its yawl configuration means the Caledonia Yawl can be easily hove-to in a strong wind. (Photo: Kathy Mansfield.)*

BOTTOM RIGHT *Scalloway was built by Frank Schofield, who reintroduced many of the features of the original Shetland boats. (Photo: Kathy Mansfield.)*

breasthooks. The thole pins for the oars were replaced by bronze rowlocks, and the tapered gunwales replaced by timbers of uniform thickness. The rig was updated too, with a sensible yawl rig replacing the huge, unmanageable dipping lugs of the original boats. It was a thorough and well-considered updating of a design that had been around for hundreds of years, making it not only suitable for modern materials but also for modern usage. This boat was to be used mainly for inshore pleasure sailing, after all, and not for fishing in the wilds of north Scotland.

Beyond those functional concerns, there was something strikingly elegant about the boat. Iain had pared the concept down to its essential components, identified the parts that mattered and reconstructed the design, omitting anything that was superfluous or unnecessary. The result was a boat that was clearly traditional and fairly shouted out its ancient lineage, and yet at the same time still managed to look thoroughly modern. It was also deceptively fast.

With so many designs available for amateur construction nowadays, it's easy to forget what a landmark the Caledonia Yawl was. For, while Iain's directory had proven there were still plenty of boatbuilders building wooden boats in Britain and that a significant proportion of them used plywood, few had bothered to take an indigenous British craft and completely reinterpret it for epoxy plywood construction. It was no more than he and others had done with so many American boats, but the fact that the principle had been applied to a British type signalled a major change in consciousness on the part of the British wooden boatbuilding scene.

'The challenge was how to evolve tradition, and how far you should go,' he says. 'It's easy to start with a Shetland boat, see ways to make it go faster and then lose the whole point. But at the same time, if you're designing a different boat for a different purpose, then it should look different too.'

Although the first of Iain's distinctly 'Scottish' designs predated his move north by two years, the Caledonia Yawl and the range of double-enders which followed soon came to be associated with Iain more than any other design of his. Partly this was because they were so different to anything else out there – there were after all pretty little pulling boats and pram dinghies aplenty, but relatively few double-ended dayboats on the market – but also, with their sweeping sheers and jaunty go-anywhere attitude, they stole the show at any gathering of small traditional boats and proved a magnet for the photographers' lenses.

Iain's timing was impeccable, too, as within a few years of the first design appearing, the new phenomenon of coastal 'raids' began (long-distance races for open boats, more of which later) for which the boats proved ideally suited. Not only did they win races, but the events attracted widespread publicity which helped promote the boats and their designer further afield. As if to confirm its standing in the pantheon of great boat designs, the Caledonia Yawl featured in a list of the 100 'best boats' compiled for the 100th issue of *Classic Boat* in October 1996, alongside designs by the likes of Charles Nicholson, William Fife and Nathanael Herreshoff. The description read: 'Certainly the boat's romantic background appeals, as does the novelty of sailing her lug yawl configuration. Above all, though, it's the feeling that, even though she is essentially a large dinghy, you could just take off on her on a madcap adventure…'

It was a view echoed by Mike O'Brien when he reviewed the boat in *WoodenBoat*, writing: 'I can't look at this boat without wanting to push her into the surf and take off.'

Iain's stay in Cork proved to be a productive time in terms of drawing boats, with the Fulmar following hot on the heels of the Caledonia Yawl, followed by the Egret (later renamed the Shearwater). But his single attempt at woodworking – carving a sign for the local Quaker Meeting

A rare shot of Iain in a tuxedo, accompanied by Welmoed, ready to sing Haydn's Creation in Cork in November 1987. (Photo: courtesy Iain Oughtred.)

House – convinced him that it would be a difficult place to build his type of boat. His request for oak was greeted with the response: 'Come back in three months' time when the wood will be nicely seasoned.' Even for a perfectionist such as Iain, that was too long a wait.

Another highlight of Iain's stay in Ireland was singing with the East Cork Choral Society. By then Welmoed had joined him ('to liven up his life'), and she joined the choir too to give a performance of Haydn's Creation at St Mary's Dominican Church in Cork on 22 November. It was one of the few occasions in his life that Iain was persuaded to wear a tuxedo.

Back in London, the 1980s housing boom was at its peak and there was no way someone in Iain's position could hope to even get a toe on the housing ladder. Priced out of the property market, he was reduced to living in a squat in a condemned house on Brookfield Road in the Hackney district of London, which in the mid-1980s was very different to the fashionable area it was to become. Living in one of the rougher parts of London during the dying years of Thatcher's Britain wasn't the most pleasant place to be as a struggling boat designer. It didn't take him long to decide that, if this was the only way he could live in London, then it wasn't worth living there at all.

Before he left, he received the call he had been expecting ever since leaving Australia twenty years before. His son Haig had been visiting family friends in Scotland and was passing through London on his way home to Sydney. He called Iain from Waterloo Station shortly before catching a train to the airport. By the time Iain got to the station, he had twenty minutes to reacquaint himself with the son he hadn't seen since he was a baby. It was hardly enough to make up for a lifetime of missed contact, but at least a connection had been made. What's more, Iain was satisfied to see that, although Haig was much more relaxed and outgoing than he was, his son did sport the same curly hair. 'He was a nice guy – the sort of guy I could imagine having a drink with and getting on with.' It would be several years before he heard from him again.

In September 1989, by necessity as much as desire, Iain was finally forced to make his long dreamed of move north first, briefly, to a Quaker community near Sheffield and then to the land of his forebears. Once again the Quaker connection came good and he heard about the leasehold of a hut in Carbeth, ten miles north of Glasgow, going for £1,000. And that he could afford. Originally built as a social experiment to provide holiday homes for working-class Glaswegians, many of the home-built huts were permanently inhabited during the Second World War by families fleeing the German bombing of the Clyde. After the war, many of them just stayed on.

It was pretty rustic and a long way from Iain's London friends network, but it was cheap, it was out of the city and, best of all, it was in Scotland. On 16 September 1989 (the day after his 50th birthday), Iain held a 'hut-warming celebration' to welcome his friends into his new home. At last, it seemed, he really had come home.

'I had been on my way to Scotland for a long time, but I kept getting stuck in London,' Iain remembers. 'When I eventually got here, I found it much easier to fit in socially than in England. The traditional music scene was classless in Scotland, whereas in England it seemed to be confined to hairy people in woolly jumpers. There were ceilidhs and singing and dancing and story-telling – it was a totally Scottish thing. I spent a lot of time learning songs and reading up about Scottish history. I felt I had found "my place".'

The wooden hut at Carbeth, near Glasgow, where Iain spent his first winter in his adopted homeland of Scotland. (Photo: courtesy Iain Oughtred.)

For the first time, too, he was able to live off the income from the sales of his plans and could devote himself entirely to his design work, without having to take random menial jobs to make ends meet. He had seven plans listed with *WoodenBoat* (two canoes, two dories, two Acorn Skiffs and the Grey Seal) bringing in a small but steady revenue, and he was selling about one plan a week himself. It was a meagre income – he later worked out that he was paying himself just £1 per hour and working sixty-plus hours per week to survive – but it was a step in the right direction.

While in Carbeth, he met a young woman by the name of Mary Fielding, who had studied architecture and, although not fully qualified, could wield a pencil and set square. After teaching her about feet and inches, curved lines and other esoteric nautical terms, Iain was able to get her to do some of the more laborious drafting, while he concentrated on the more creative work. To start with, he paid her £3 per hour – a pittance compared to a proper draughtsman's salary, but still three times as much as he himself was earning. Her salary would eventually rise to a more respectable £7.50 per hour, still a fraction of what she would have been paid as a professional draughtsman in a city practice.

Set amid a lush panoply of trees and ferns, the huts at Carbeth looked idyllic from the outside, but they suffered from chronic damp on the inside and, because they were not officially classed as habitations, didn't have electricity. Iain worked by candles and oil lamp instead – usually working 10–12 hours a day, six days a week. Welmoed came to visit and the two of them attempted to double glaze the windows with sheets of plastic, but far from keeping the cold out it seemed only to keep the damp in. The plastic also made it impossible to open the windows and let in fresh air.

After a few months, Iain decided that the hut was more picturesque than practical, and sold it (making a handsome profit of £600), moving into a shared flat in Edinburgh. There, he went through a succession of workshops, starting at the city docks, where someone was attempting to make a business restoring old yachts (including the Robert Clark-designed *Mercy Jane*), and then on to a converted church in neighbouring Leith, where a friend of a friend was building a small aircraft which Iain later got to fly in. He eventually found a more long-term

ABOVE *Iain's BMW Biggles was a faithful companion and accompanied him to Ireland. (Photo: courtesy Welmoed Bouhuys.)*

ABOVE RIGHT *The early 1990s were a productive time for Iain, who had by then moved to Roslin Glen, near Edinburgh. (Photo: courtesy Iain Oughtred.)*

space on a farm that was being converted at Bonnyrigg, eight miles south of Edinburgh, and moved into a flat on a small estate at nearby Roslin Glen.

His new home was big enough to fit two drawing boards, one for Iain and one for Mary, which was more conducive to work and approximated the design studio he had long dreamed of. There was even space enough to park his motorbike indoors, much to his delight and Mary's despair. The flat was dark, but not half as damp as the hut at Carbeth, and there was a caravan in the garden where Welmoed could stay whenever she pitched up for one of her regular visits. Nearby was one of the sites claimed for Robert the Bruce's cave, where the Scottish king holed up and plotted his campaign against the English, something of which Iain was inordinately proud.

There was a downside to life at Roslin Glen, however, as while living there his asthma returned with a vengeance. It may have been triggered by the damp of those Scottish winters or epoxy fumes or, according to a professional dowser who paid a visit, the energy from a major ley line that passed through the house. Whatever the cause, it was enough to knock Iain flat on his back and put him in hospital for nine days.

His work continued to be productive, thanks in part to Mary, who proved adept at boatbuilding as well as draughting. Continuing his policy of, whenever possible, building his designs in order to ensure the plans worked as well in real life as on paper, Iain started building two of his latest creations: the 11ft 6in Ptarmigan (later renamed the Guillemot) and the 6ft 8in Feather Pram. Both boats evolved from existing designs in response to feedback from clients wanting bigger or smaller versions – the Ptarmigan was an elongated version of Iain's popular Puffin design, while the Feather was a shortened, traditional Pram.

By then, Iain had a tried and tested approach to developing new designs. First he would look at as many boats of that type and size as he could find – in the case of the Ptarmigan, it was still largely a case of looking at the work of Phil Bolger, Gardner and Peter Culler, as 90% of the design books on his shelf were by American writers. He would then draw up a table with the relevant boats' principal dimensions – freeboard, depth, strength of sheer, sail area, displacement – which he then averaged out. That gave him a median base to refer to. If his design

For several years, Iain was a regular fixture at the Wooden Boat Show in Greenwich, here photographed with the new Mouse pram c1990. (Photo: courtesy Iain Oughtred.)

was significantly different in any area, he would know not necessarily that it was wrong but that it would have different characteristics, possibly desirable, possibly not.

'There are inevitably odd boats that are significantly different to average,' he says, 'and I will think about those and whether the designer has done it for some particular reason – for example, wanting more stability and less sail area because it's going to a particularly windy place. Sometimes, there's no apparent reason at all. Generally, I may well be aiming for a lighter hull or bigger sail area, bearing in mind that most of my designs are lighter boats for having fun with, whereas many of the original designs are for working boats carrying large loads of fish.'

Once he had examined all the data on existing designs, he put it out of his mind as much as possible while he drew his own boat. If it was a brand new project, the first sketch was usually a profile and sail plan, which he drew on a scrap of tracing paper – about A3 size (tabloid size in the US). That got worked on, and probably rubbed out and redrawn repeatedly, until Iain was happy with the look of it, and only then would he draw the lines at a scale of 1:8 (ie 1½in:1ft), before moving on to the construction plans and the sail plan. If it was a boat in an existing series of designs, such as the Scottish double-enders, then he might start straight off working on film – but only if it was a genre he was thoroughly familiar with.

Building the boat for real not only helped Iain flesh out the details of the plans and add the high level of detail for which he was known, but it could sometimes lead to fairly drastic changes in the design itself. Once the prototype Ptarmigan was complete, for instance, he realized that the sheer was a little bolder in the finished boat than he had anticipated in the drawings, so he was able to flatten it out in subsequent drawings and lower the stem by about ¾in – a small change but one which made all the difference to his hyper-critical eye. The result was a handsome dayboat which, first as the Ptarmigan and then the Guillemot, would go on to become his best-selling design, with more than 200 plans sold since 1991.

Iain took both the prototype Ptarmigan and Feather Pram to the 1992 Greenwich Wooden Boat Show, and the reaction was strikingly different to that when Iain and Fabian had first stood 'in the wind and the rain' at Southampton all those years ago. Whereas at Southampton, visitors were simply amazed to see wooden boats there at all and showed their ignorance by

Colin Galloway at the helm of his Whilly Boat, the smallest in Iain's range of Shetland-style double-enders. (Photo: Kathy Mansfield.)

the naivety of their questions, the Greenwich show nine years later was a true gathering of the cognoscenti. And, unlike the first year when one fibreglass boat somehow managed to slip through the net (the traditionally-styled Kittiwake, built by Roger Wilkinson), this time there really were only wooden boats at the show.

'It was completely different to ten years before,' Iain remembers. 'People at Greenwich were asking sensible questions – like what types of wood the boats were made of, instead of simply whether they were made of wood. People were already more knowledgeable and had a better idea of what they wanted and what you could do with these boats. That's when I knew that things had really developed.'

His new range of Scottish double-enders had proven popular, and the Caledonia Yawl was soon followed by the 16ft 6in Ness Boat (which would later evolve into the Tirrik) and the 14ft 6in Whilly Boat (later to become the Whilly Tern). These were capable, seaworthy designs, drawn very much with rowing in mind. For himself, however, Iain had something more exciting in mind. He wanted

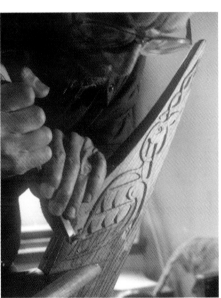

a flatter, more stable hull, which might not row as well but could take a bit more sail and, ultimately, sail faster. He wanted nothing less than a Shetland speedster!

Iain drew the Ness Yawl in 1992, but the design sat around for several months, until a yacht-racing friend of Mary's called Mike finally called Iain's bluff and said, 'Are you going to build this boat, or what? If you are, I'd like to help!'

It was all the prompting he needed. Within a few weeks the backbone of the Ness Yawl was set up in a room loaned to him by some Quaker friends, Jane and Roger, who had a big house in Penicuik, a few miles west of Roslin Glen. With no door opening onto the outside, the plan was to take the window out of its frame and carry the boat out that way. As the boat grew, however, Jane became increasingly convinced that the enormous-looking vessel taking shape in her room couldn't possibly fit out of the narrow window aperture, and it took a great deal of measuring and remeasuring to persuade her that it would work. And well she might have worried. As the boat came together, Iain couldn't resist tweaking her a little bit, changing a line curve here and stretching a line there.

Building the prototype Ness Yawl, with the able assistance of his drawing assistant Mary (pictured, bottom left). Jeanie Henderson was essentially a souped-up and elongated version of the Whilly Boat. (Photos: courtesy Iain Oughtred.)

'I got a bit experimental with that one,' he says. 'I flattened her out a bit more when I was designing her and then, when we were actually building her, I took a good look at the bottom and flattened it a bit more. She ended up long, flat and broad – almost a planing shape. It was an interesting experiment, but I think I exaggerated it a bit much, which made the boat more sensitive to weight. The result was that, with four people on board, she was low in water and dragging her arse – but two up, she was dead fast.' Needless to say, all these 'exaggerations' were ironed out and moderated in the published drawings – though you can be sure that Iain has the more 'extreme' version stashed away somewhere, should someone feel the urge to be wild and crazy.

It was while building the prototype Ness Yawl that Iain first started experimenting with different plywoods. For years it almost went without saying that the only true marine ply was Brunzeel ply from Holland, which was manufactured to the exacting BS 1088 standard (which includes such requirements as boil-proof glue, no voids in the veneers and no knots on the outer veneers). Like most marine ply, however, Brunzeel was usually faced with gaboon, mahogany or teak, which came from questionable (ie unsustainable) sources, and in any case were not in the least bit Scottish. The solution was to glue some elm veneers to a gaboon core, using vacuum bagging. As the thickness of the elm veneer varied from $\frac{1}{16}$in to $\frac{1}{32}$in, however, it was hard to gauge how much glue to apply, and for months after Iain had to slide more glue into the lifting patches using feeler gauges.

Finally, the great day came and the boat was finished and, whereas most boats have a launch party, the Ness Yawl had an 'oot-the-windae' (out the window) party – or a 'defenestration'. Mary, who was famous for baking suitable cakes for suitable occasions, turned up with a suitably-shaped 'oot-the-windae' cake. The window was duly taken off the window frame, the boat lifted by the assembled friends and eased out onto the lawn. Iain named her *Jeanie*

After several months' gestation, Jeanie Henderson *emerges from the womb for her 'oot-the-windae' party. (Photo: courtesy Iain Oughtred.)*

Henderson in honour of his mother, whose ancestors would have seen similar boats going about their daily lives in the Orkneys.

True to his word, *Jeanie Henderson* turned out to be a seriously fast boat, as well as seriously hairy to sail. For several years, she took the Scottish wooden boat scene by storm, as Iain and his freakish steed became a regular fixture at the Traditional Boat Festival in Portsoy. On one famous occasion, they lapped the rest of the fleet and were sent off to sail an extra round of the course. It was also a triumph for British and, more specifically, Scottish small boat heritage, so long in the shadow of its American counterpart. Every Caledonia Yawl, Ness Boat, Whilly Boat or Ness Yawl that was launched paid tribute to a unique Scottish tradition and helped ensure it was not forgotten.

It was a pivotal time for Iain's career, and in a two-page CV written for the French magazine *Chasse Marée*, he sums up his position with typical self-deprecation:

'As always, [I] spend a lot of time refining and perfecting the stock plans, planning new designs that there will never be time for, and complaining about the lack of time. To alleviate this problem, [I] am employing part-time workers – with some success. There are few with the necessary skill, who will work for very low wages. But [there are] some who are fascinated by the boats, and prefer it to a proper job.

'I now sell three plans per week. The royalties from ten designs sold by *WoodenBoat* make it possible to survive. If things improve, I will be in danger of earning a taxable income.

'Future ambitions: some small-boat racing; cruising the west coast of Scotland; building a trimaran; designing shallow-draught cruising yachts, canoe-yawls, training boats and racing

With its workboat pedigree, the Ness Yawl has seagoing capability, as Wahoo *shows, sailing off Portsoy in Scotland. (Photo: Kathy Mansfield.)*

The Traditional Boat
Festival at Portsoy
provided a rallying point
for Scottish wooden
boats, including several
of Iain's designs. (Photo:
Kathy Mansfield.)

dinghies. And finding time for other interests: music and instruments, reading and writing; calligraphy; building an ecological house; model-making.'

It was while he was building the Ness Yawl that Iain received the second contact from his son. He had spent all day at the workshop and came back in the evening to his flat at Roslin Glen to find a note stuck under his door. It read simply: 'Just passing by, sorry to miss you. See you another time.' He still had Haig's girlfriend's number from their previous encounter and eventually tracked her down to a flat in London, only to discover that it was Haig's last night in Britain. He would be flying back to Australia at 8am the following morning. It was too late for Iain to drive down to meet him as he had hoped and, instead, he had to content himself with a half-hour chat on the phone at about 2am. It was only years later he discovered that his son had been living just down the road in Edinburgh for several months.

'We had a good chat that night, but when I woke up the next day I felt depressed about it. I had always thought that, even though I wasn't there for him when he was little, one day he would come looking for me and would ask me about my life and I would ask him about his, and we would get to know each other. But I realized then it wasn't going to be like that. He had grown up without me and didn't need me – I wasn't a part of his life and probably never would be.'

IAIN'S TOP TEN

First published in *Classic Boat*, October 1996

International 10 Square Metre Canoe

From the little paddling/sailing canoes of a hundred years ago, a long process of evolution led to the 10 Square Metre. The 17ft (5.23m) hull is now one-design, but the rig is open; you can do what you like with your 10 square metres. The IC is faster than any other single-hander. And she's got real style...

Three Cheers

Dick Newick's 46ft (14m) *Three Cheers* design, with her strong sheer, longish buoyant ends and moderate mast height, has less potential for high speed than more extreme racers, but possesses a more sea-kindly motion, and so had dramatic success in the transatlantic races. *Three Cheers* is a classic.

Tioga and Bounty

A boat designed in the 1930s has to be out of date in some way, but if I had the kind of money for a 57ft 6in (17.5m) vessel, it would be Herreshoff's *Tioga* and *Bounty*. Francis had true artistic genius; the best of his creations show a magnificent harmony.

B14E

The Australians seem to be miles ahead in the development of light, fast boats. Julian Bethwaite's B14E is a classic with a more interesting performance than anything else, on a relatively small and lightweight hull.

Presto

One of the great misconceptions commonly held is that a deep draught hull is necessary for seagoing ability and safety. Munroe in the early 1900s designed the 41ft (12.5m) *Presto*, an attractive and handy vessel, easily managed by a small crew, and able to cruise many shallow coastal areas, yet face up to the heaviest seas.

30 Square Metre Class

The skerry cruisers of the 1930s and 1940s were the most graceful and elegant sailing yachts ever. For performance and handling, no modern craft can touch them. Knud Reimers was the most successful designer; his *Darling* exemplifies his artistry.

Norma

Two things fascinate me about canoe yawls: their friendly character, and how they evolved from the late 19th century through light open canoes to half-deck mini-cruisers to ballasted dayboats and finally into cruising yachts. No modern designer has yet achieved the character, the grace of line and the perfect proportions of the canoe yawls by George Holmes and Albert Strange. The 24ft 5in (7.4m) *Norma* is a work of art.

Black Skimmer

I like the simplicity of the American sharpies. The flat bottom and sides have limitations, but Philip Bolger here has applied his 'instant boat' method to produce an inexpensive, light, 25ft 3in (7.7m) cruising boat which is surprisingly fast and handy. The 'Solent lug' rig makes it easy to raise and lower the mast, and safer in a hard breeze with reefed foresail.

Wren

The Wren from the Clyde Canoe Club is typical of the decked sailing canoe developed from John MacGregor's Rob Roy designs, used for some adventurous cruising and, with ever-increasing sail area, for racing. Most rigs had fully-battened sails, often gunter-rigged, and were fitted with complex reefing gear that could be operated from the cockpit.

Ness Yawl

Many boats inspired by traditional working craft are not particularly exciting to sail; this one is. With the 19ft 2in (5.8m) *Jeanie Henderson*, I wanted to push the evolution of the Shetland type to its logical conclusion. She is light, broad and flat aft for semi-displacement and planing performance, and has proved unbeatable in races for 'classic' boats.

chapter 6

THE EPOXY CONNECTION

AIN'S NEXT MOVE WAS, symbolically, further north. Sveinung Skåtun, a woodworker friend, had told him about a space that was available in an old stone building near the harbour in Findhorn. It seemed like an ideal set-up for the peripatetic builder/designer: a place where he could have a studio as well as a workshop, looking out onto a picturesque harbour, with all the wild, unfettered North Sea on the other side of the sand bar. It was every bit the 'small shop in a beautiful setting on the water' that Iain had described as his ambition a decade before in his book *Wooden Boatbuilding in Britain.*

Once an important port with a thriving shipbuilding industry and trading links with Scandinavia, Findhorn boasted a yacht club with rather grand premises overlooking the bay. Although Iain had little in common with most of the sailors there, the club's facilities – including an efficient rescue service – did give him the opportunity to try out some modern dinghies. For, while he had done very little serious racing since leaving Australia, he was still fascinated by the process of achieving speed on the water and extracting the optimum performance from a hull design.

Thus it was that, approaching his 60th birthday, Iain could be found dashing across the bay first on an RS600 ('a clever reefing system, but the boat hasn't been developed or refined enough prior to going into production') and then a 29er ('well thought out, though I could suggest four or five minor refinements'). And he made sure the club rescue boat stayed alert by indulging in a little 'swimming practice', although he insists he always righted the boat without assistance.

The town had the added benefit of being home to the Findhorn Foundation, the spiritual/ecology centre where Iain had met Sveinung and, years before, Welmoed. As well as offering courses in everything from yoga to sustainable architecture, the Foundation had its own eco-village (mainly a bunch of caravans with a few timber frame buildings scattered among them) which had developed into a lively alternative community. Although the internal politics of the place were somewhat volatile at that time, the Foundation was a good substitute for the social and cultural stimulation Iain had enjoyed while living in Edinburgh – a place where he could meet like-minded people and develop his non-boating interests.

One of those was the daily Taizé meeting. First thing every morning, a group of mainly community members met in the beautifully-crafted Universal Hall to sing devotional songs inspired by the Christian monastic order of the same name in France. The sound of all those voices singing in rounds and harmonizing made each individual feel a part of something much bigger, as well as

The wizard of Findhorn. Iain is master of ceremonies at the burning of a paper birlinn, built by him. (Photo: courtesy Iain Oughtred.)

being incredibly soothing. It was a profoundly spiritual yet non-religious experience which suited Iain to the core and, for a while, it took precedence over his Quaker visits.

Iain's movement further north was interpreted by some, rather unkindly, as an attempt to escape the ever-increasing cost of housing in the south. While there may have been an element of truth in this (particularly his initial move out of London) more than anything it was driven by a growing devotion to his adopted homeland of Scotland and a desire to immerse himself deeper into its culture. Indeed, as he gradually developed a Scottish burr and increasingly peppered his conversation with Scottish expressions such as 'wee', there were many who assumed that he was Scottish. It was an impression he did nothing to contradict.

It was an opportune time to complete one of his many ongoing projects: his second book. Despite the resurgence of interest in wooden boats in the UK, there were still few practical books for amateur boatbuilders to refer to and almost nothing relating to clinker plywood construction. It was a clear omission which, ever since he built the first Acorn in his workshop on the Thames, Iain had been meaning to rectify. To this end, he had carefully documented the building of both the Ptarmigan and the Ness Yawl, and by the time both projects were finished he had amassed enough pictures to illustrate a book.

After an abortive attempt to publish the book in 1995 while he was in Edinburgh, the final version of the *Clinker Plywood Boatbuilding Manual* was published in 1998 (and successfully so, as the co-published edition with WoodenBoat Books now has over 12,000 copies in print). It was, of course, a methodical piece of work, with a great deal of background information and step-by-step photography of building a boat (in fact, several boats, as the photos came from a variety of sources as well as the Ptarmigan and the Ness Yawl). It would be nice to think that the *Clinker Plywood Boatbuilding Manual* was an uncharacteristically businesslike attempt by Iain to fill a 'gap in the market' and thereby drum up some much-needed revenue. Anyone who knows him, however, will know that it was far more likely to have been driven by a serious desire to promote the greater cause of wooden boatbuilding and traditional designs.

The title of the book was significant for, while to most boatbuilders the term 'clinker plywood' was effectively synonymous with 'epoxy ply', Iain was still holding out against the near monopoly of the 'sticky stuff'. Indeed, in his section on glues (pointedly subheaded 'There are Other Glues'), he picks up the theme first mooted in his previous book *Wooden Boatbuilding in Britain*: 'It should be obvious from the above that the advent of epoxy has not actually brought about a great revolution in wooden boatbuilding, as is often claimed,' he wrote, before extolling the virtues of traditional glues. There then follows page after page of wonderfully clear instruction for what appears to be mainly epoxy-ply construction, including extensive use of filleting and an illustration for an epoxy fibreglass 'weld', or plank joint.

Yet, interviewed ten years later, Iain remained adamant that our obsession with epoxy is just a result of hype: 'I first used epoxy when I was building the Acorn Skiff, just because I wanted to see if it was as good as everyone said it was. The resorcinol I used on my first dory had suffered glue failure when the laminated stem fell apart – it was the first time I had experienced that and was probably due to the freezing cold conditions when I built her. The gap-filling properties of epoxy appealed to me, although I wasn't doing fancy filleting at the time. But I have no interest in epoxy sheathing, and I don't like epoxy that much – that's why I say more in my book about other glues.

'I don't agree with the prevailing philosophy that the use of epoxy has totally transformed boatbuilding – that's absolutely prattle. It's brought about a slight variation on what we've been doing for years and years using resorcinol and Cascamite type glues. Epoxy has simplified a few things, but I think just as many boats would have been built without it.'

It's a view that goes against just about everything you read or hear anywhere else. Every person contacted while researching this book – be it builder, designer or journalist – agreed that epoxy not only transformed wooden boatbuilding but was probably largely responsible for the whole revival in the first place. Indeed, one builder said it was 'unimaginable' that the revival would have taken place on the scale it did without epoxy. Another suggested that it was an indication of Iain's high standard of craftsmanship that he could contemplate building plywood boats using traditional glues, which require exceptionally well-fitting joints. Most people, he said, rely heavily on epoxy to help them fill imperfect joints.

The yachting journalist Adrian Morgan described the influence of epoxy in an article about the 'second-wave' plywood revolution (the first being the pre-glassfibre phase in the 1950s): 'Today, a new generation, for a different reason, is turning against glassfibre and discovering that plywood panels, in varying widths, can produce good looking boats with some of the old-fashioned integrity of solid timber. The pioneering work of the Gougeon Brothers in particular has probably made this possible. Resorcinol may be better, but epoxy is a forgiving, if controversial, glue whose versatility overrides its expense. It enables the bodger to get away with it, and the skilled to produce shells that float on the dew with the strength of a steel girder.'

It is ironic that the man who has probably contributed more than any other designer towards epoxy ply construction – including pioneering it in those very early days through articles in *WoodenBoat* and elsewhere and producing dozens of detailed designs to be built in the medium – should be so apparently ambivalent about its use now. One possible explanation is a personal one: using the glue can trigger Iain's asthma, so it can be quite debilitating. But the reason is more likely because he feels that the focus on epoxy somehow detracts attention from the star of the show: wood. If wood is dependent on epoxy for its existence, then that demeans the very essence of what Iain's work is all about: traditional materials, craftsmanship and integrity. And, after all, this was supposed to be a wooden boat revival, not a celebration of a synthetic,

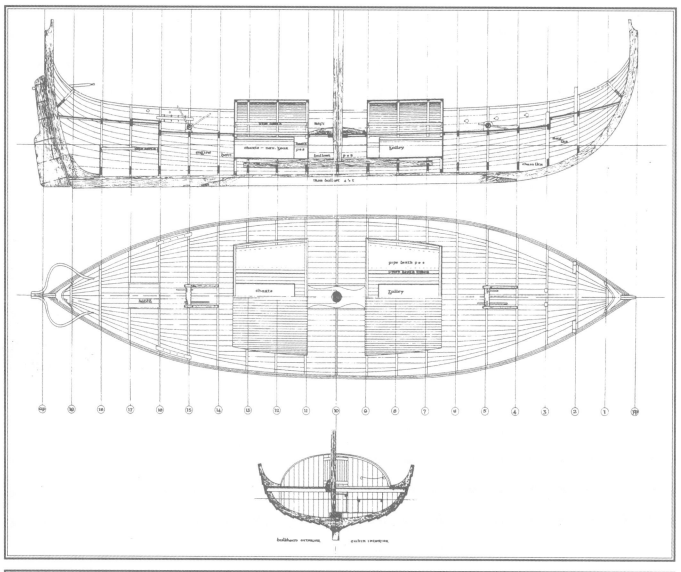

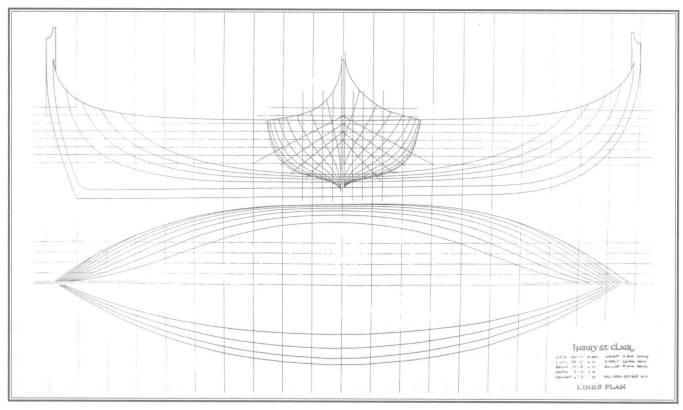

henry st clair

LINES PLAN

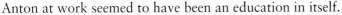

oil-based glue. In practice, however, Iain himself admits that the majority of his designs are probably built from epoxy ply and that he only very occasionally hears about them being built using anything else.

Iain's time at Findhorn proved to be one of the most settled in his life, something which was reflected in his work output. Several new designs emerged, including an unusually contemporary-looking rowing boat, the Snipefish, which looked as if it was specifically designed to tackle the surf breaking over the bar at the entrance of Findhorn Bay. He also indulged in his fascination with prams by designing his fourth, the 8ft Humble Bee, named after a fat bumble bee that came buzzing into the room just when he was wondering what to call the boat. And he oversa a workshop building a 13ft Acorn Skiff, organized by builder/instructor Anton Fitzpatrick. Watching Anton at work seemed to have been an education in itself.

'I was dead impressed with the way he came to a strange place he'd never been to before, pulled all the wood and bits of gear out of the back of the van, and built a boat with a bunch of complete strangers. Each person had very different levels of experience, intelligence and abilities, but he was able to very quickly work out how fast they were, how hard he could push them, and how quickly they could learn, and get them working together and building a boat within a week. It was pretty rough boatbuilding, but he was a bloody good teacher. I used to sometimes think I should be doing workshops, but after Anton demonstrated how it should be done, I realized I couldn't do it that way.'

At the end of the course, Iain was left with the bare hull, which he cleaned up and fitted out for his own use. The resulting boat, called *Hoolet*, featured on the cover of the very first issue of *Water Craft*, a specialist magazine devoted to small boat building. The photographer Kathy Mansfield was so enamoured by the little skiff that she ended up buying it from Iain – his boats have that effect on people.

Then, in 1995, Iain received a commission for his largest design to date: a replica of a 14th-century Scottish galley. The 60ft *Henry St Clair* was intended to re-enact the voyage of the explorer of the same name, who is said to have sailed to America in 1398. With the 600th anniversary of the voyage coming up, a team was set up to raise the £200,000 needed for the replica, and Iain was commissioned to draw the lines and build a scale model of the boat. The only other Scottish galley (or birlinn) to have been built in modern times was the 40ft *Aileach*, designed by Colin Mudie and launched in Ireland in 1991. Despite the ship having sailed around the north of Scotland to the Faroe Islands and garnered acres of publicity along the way, Iain was deeply scathing about the authenticity of the design and the quality of its construction. He had to admit, however, that there was very little material evidence, let alone any reliable lines, to base a replica on.

'There was good information from research that has been done on stone carvings of galleys, and a lot of good work has been done on Viking ships at Roskilde in Denmark. The galleys were basically the same as the Viking ships, except that the hulls were more drawn out and finer at either

The Henry St Clair *was a 60ft Scottish galley intended to commemorate the 600th anniversary of a voyage to America. Iain designed the ship and built a detailed model of it, but the full-size version was never built.*

end – and the Scots added a rudder on the stern. Most of the details of construction and rigging came from Viking boats. But that's about it. Once you've studied the carvings and looked at the Viking ships and learned what you can from them, then you have to draw the ship as best you can from the information you have. There will inevitably be grey areas, but you have to make it look as convincing as possible. Where you cannot be certain it's authentic, it has to be credible.'

The St Clair project foundered due to lack of funds (and, no doubt, time), but the drawings show Iain's uncanny ability to develop an elegant hull shape from the most obscure traditional references, while still retaining something distinctly 'Oughtred-ish' about them. They are also exquisite drawings in their own right.

His research came in useful a few years later when he was asked to design another galley, this time for GalGael, a community group based in Glasgow. Led by the charismatic Colin MacLeod – once known as the 'Birdman of Pollok' after he spent nine days up a tree in protest against the building of a motorway through Pollok Park – the organization ran craft-based workshops for the disadvantaged in one of the most deprived areas of Scotland. They had already built a 30ft galley and had their sights set on a 48ft flagship in which they could sail around Scotland and raise awareness of their work.

Drawing on his earlier work for the St Clair project, Iain made a scale model of a 48ft which, if built, would be the first 'proper' galley to be built for 300 years. The project suffered a major setback when MacLeod died in 2005, but eventually recovered its momentum. In the summer of 2008 came the news that the Forestry Commission had offered not only to donate the timber but also to cut it to size. It would be a fine tribute to Colin, a man who did so much to help others, if the GalGael galley was built, as well as being a significant step in Scottish maritime history.

By this time, the wooden boat revival was well under way throughout Europe, with large fleets of traditional boats of all sizes attending maritime festivals in Portsmouth and Bristol in the UK, as well as Brest and Douarnenez in France, Risør in Norway and Flensburg in Germany, not to mention Scotland's own 'wee' gathering in Portsoy. One of the most important developments in the small boat scene was the creation of a series of cruising races for small craft. The concept was the brainchild of the French event organizer Charles-Henri Le Moing and his company Albacore, who had previously organized a number of catamaran races in the Philippines. Because the original events combined racing with adventure cruises between the islands, with crews camping on beaches at each stop, they became known as 'raids'.

The first 'raid' to be run in Europe was on the Douro River in Portugal in 1996, and the boats had changed from sports catamarans to traditional 'sail and oar' type craft. As the concept evolved, the races became increasingly dominated by the emerging breed of contemporary epoxy-ply designs, of which Iain was one of the leading exponents. Indeed, the winner of the second Douro River Raid was a Caledonia Yawl built by Frank Schofield and navigated by none other than Iain's old friend Jamie Clay. Of all Iain's designs, the Caledonia Yawl combined the key ingredients needed in a successful 'raid' boat: ability under oar and sail, seaworthiness to cope with variable sea conditions and, last but not least, speed.

Not surprisingly, when Charles-Henri was asked to organize a similar event in Scotland in 2000, Iain was one of the first people he got in touch with.

'I had heard a great deal about him and knew his boats through the Douro raids, but I had never met him in person. So I arranged to have lunch with him at Findhorn, where he

had a nice workshop by the harbour,' says Charles-Henri. 'When I arrived, there was a huge sea coming through the harbour entrance and, unbelievably, a small boat rowing over the waves and coping very well. It was Iain. He was wearing a funny hat and what looked like home-made wooden glasses and didn't correspond at all to my idea of a naval architect. He was very supportive of the idea of a raid in Scotland, however, and said it was just what was needed. It was Iain's connections and influence, along with the financial support of Bill Sylvester [chief executive of the Inverness & Nairn Enterprise agency], that made the first event possible.'

Not only did Iain lend his support, but he was an enthusiastic participant in that first Great Glen Raid and the ones that followed, more often than not with his trusty friend Welmoed providing shore support in a variety of colourful vehicles. For the first 'raid', he borrowed a Ness Yawl and joined a fleet of 42 small boats travelling from Fort William on the west coast through the Caledonian Canal to Inverness and Fort George on the east coast. Comprising several long days' sailing and rowing through dramatic Highland scenery and subject to sudden katabatic winds shooting down the hillsides at up to 30 knots, it was not a trip for the faint-hearted. But, as Iain suggested in a report on the first event for *Classic Boat* magazine, that was what made the event a 'raid' rather than just a cruise. He wrote:

'One of the good things about racing, even this fairly informal kind, is that it encourages sailors to push the boat to the edge – to carry a little too much sail, to push the boat a little harder than really seems sensible. This may seem to be verging on the irresponsible, but it does force you to learn very quickly the boat's potential. It also trains the crew in seamanship and survival tactics, in ways which they might otherwise take years to learn – if at all. The skills and confidence gained will add enormously to the boat's safety and the crew's enjoyment on future occasions when sudden squalls or difficult conditions turn up.'

The Ness Yole No Name *puts in a strong performance under oar at the 2003 Blekinge Archipelago Raid. (Photo: Erwan Quemere/Abacore.)*

Charles-Henri ran the Scottish event for three years before it was taken over by a local group and rebranded Sail Caledonia, as it has been run every year since. Meanwhile, the Albacore team had moved on to pastures new and had launched a new series of raids in southern Sweden. The Blekinge Archipelago Raid took place over 85 miles of some of the most unspoilt coastline in Europe and included two exposed legs to reach Sweden's southernmost islands. As in the Scottish raid, Iain's Caledonia and Ness Yawls proved the ideal boats for the terrain and performed well in both events, only beaten by the more modern (and rather less pretty) designs of French naval architect Gilles Montaubin.

'When I first saw Iain's designs at the second Douro raid I was a bit reticent,' says Charles-Henri. 'I thought they were too much a copy of old boats. But bit by bit I noticed how Iain had evolved the shapes to be more modern and faster. His boats are light, finely-shaped and seaworthy. In the end, I was astonished by their performance. There is no equivalent in France. We have François Vivier [a prolific designer of traditionally-inspired small boats] who designs good boats, but they are just copies of boats his grandfather would have sailed. He is not original – you can't compare him to Iain. Other designers copy old boats, but Iain has evolved the designs – he is the only one to do this.'

So impressed was Charles-Henri by Iain's work that he commissioned a Ness Yawl to be built for himself – a significant endorsement from a man who has seen most of the best-known and quite a few unknown small boats perform in a huge variety of circumstances. He did,

Commissioned by raid creator Charles-Henri Le Moing, Alba has been a fixture at several of the events. (Photo: Nic Compton.)

The sloop-rigged Jeanie II *shows her pace next to the yawl-rigged* Wahoo. *Iain now favours the sloop rig.* (Photo: Kathy Mansfield.)

however, make a couple of significant changes to the original, which he believed would make for a more seakindly vessel. The first was to add about 100lb of ballast to improve stability and the other was to partially deck over the boat, leaving an oval-shaped cockpit with side decks. *Alba*, as the boat was called, took part in the second Great Glen Raid with her builder Kees Prins at the helm. As Charles-Henri readily admits, she has the distinction of being the only one of Iain's designs to have capsized in any of the raids he has organized!

For Iain, participating in events such as the Portsoy festival and the Great Glen Raid provided him with an opportunity to push his boats to the limits and see how they responded. Using this practical experience, he was then able to develop the designs in more detail, fine-tuning the rig and other aspects. Racing the boats in such challenging conditions gave him insights which he wouldn't have had without that competitive element.

It was while sailing in the first Great Glen Raid that Iain had something of a revelation. Up until then he had always assumed that the yawl configuration would be more sensible on a boat the size of the Ness Yawl. The rig, he reasoned, allowed the helmsman to heave-to with only the mizzen set while setting or reefing the main, while in windy conditions it allowed you to sail safely under jib and mizzen alone. He was therefore somewhat apprehensive sailing his single-masted lug-rigged *Gruoch* alone on what he knew might be a breezy stretch of water.

'Halfway down Loch Ness, the wind suddenly came in quite fresh, gusting about 30 knots. I needed to take in a couple reefs quite quickly, but I had no mizzen to heave-to. I thought I would have to drop everything and drift, while I waited for the wind to change. While I was sitting there trying to figure it out, the boat just quietly sat there, patiently hove-to all by herself, while she waited for me to get sorted. So I took a couple of reefs in, quickly bore away and away we

Eun Na Mara's sweet lines and commodious hull (for a 20-footer!) show that Iain's skill isn't confined to small boats.

went. It was as simple as that! Afterwards, I thought, what was that mizzen for, after all that? With the extra sail, extra boom and the ridiculous laminated tillers – what was it for?'

He still recommends the yawl rig for larger boats, such as his own Caledonia Yawl, but says for himself he wouldn't bother with it. He understands that some people like the idea of it and just think it 'looks cool'.

Although best known for his open boat designs, Iain occasionally received commissions for bigger boats. In 1997 he was approached by psychotherapist Avery Brice wanting a pocket cruiser of the type popularized by designers such as Albert Strange and George Holmes at the beginning of the last century. Unlike most of Iain's previous work, it seems to have been very much a joint project. Avery had a clear idea of what he wanted and presented Iain with a clear set of criteria which Iain then had to translate into a viable boat. The main battle ground was the height of the coachroof, with the owner pleading for plenty of headroom below decks and the designer unwilling to sacrifice the line of the boat for mere creature comforts.

The result was the 19ft 9in *Eun Na Mara*, a pretty double-ender which, with its gaff yawl rig and sturdy (rather than graceful) good looks, is in many ways untypical of Iain's work. One ingenious feature is the double centreboards, which do away with the need for a single centreboard in the middle of the boat, breaking up the accommodation. Instead, the two boards are located on either side of the keel, with the cases neatly incorporated in the cabin furniture. The design has proven especially popular in Australia, where Iain's plans are sold through Duck Flat Wooden Boats online store.

The 1990s were a difficult time for many boatbuilders, not only because of the uncertain economic climate but because of new legislation imposed by the European Union (EU). The

Recreational Craft Directive (RCD) was intended to standardize building regulations across the EU, so that companies could build boats to one set of rules rather than having to adapt them to comply with the regulations of each individual country they were sold in. The first directive, introduced in Britain in 1996 and made obligatory two years later, was mainly concerned with safety issues, such as making sure boats had sufficient buoyancy and weren't liable to capsize. This was followed in 2006 by a second tranche of rules focused on environmental issues, such as exhaust emissions and sound pollution.

The new regulations were welcomed by big manufacturers keen to open up new markets, but for small boatbuilders, whose customers were mostly fairly local anyway, they added a huge extra layer of bureaucracy, not to mention expense. A conservative industry at the best of times, there was widespread anger at Brussels meddling in an area that had until then remained largely unregulated. There was also a widespread fear among purists that traditional boat types, despite having proven themselves through decades or even centuries of use, might not pass the strict standards set by the RCD, or that they might need to be altered to comply and thereby lose their essential character.

For Iain and other designers like him, the danger was very real. At the very least, it would have required all his designs to be redrawn to comply with the directive; at worst, it could have spelled the end of his career. After much protest, however, the EU made some significant concessions and excluded several types of craft, including 'original, and individual replicas of historical craft designed before 1950, built predominantly with original materials'. It also excluded boats built 'for own use', provided they were not sold in the EU within five years of completion.

The ruling meant that all Iain's designs for amateur construction were exempt. It also placed an unexpected premium on boats which could claim to be 'replicas of historical craft', a definition which was loose enough to be exploited by any professional wooden boatbuilders who could claim some kind of pedigree for his/her design – be it a Bristol Channel pilot cutter or an American dory.

While Iain's designs were clearly in the ascendancy, his own personal situation had become more fraught. His trusty helper Mary, who had taken on much of the draughting work for the past ten years and freed him to use his time more creatively, had found other work and Iain was unable to find anyone to replace her – perhaps not surprisingly given the rates he could afford to pay. A few years later, she died unexpectedly, leaving an unstoppable hole in the lives of her family and friends. For one thing, there would be no one to bake suitably-shaped cakes for suitable occasions.

In a letter to Charles-Henri on 20 June 1999, Iain wrote that his situation had changed little in the past seven years, apart from a 'better working place' and a 'determination to keep at least two boats operational'. He then went on to list 12 designs he had drawn since 1992. But he also made it clear that, despite this impressive output, he still hadn't achieved his life's work:

'Most of my frustrated ambitions are still waiting to be fulfilled. I need a draughtsman, a boatbuilder, a part-time secretary. So that I can concentrate on the fun jobs – new designs and prototypes. But [I] can not afford to pay these people.'

IAIN ON SPRIT RIGS

(Extract from *WoodenBoat* May/June 1987)

The spritsail, in its basic small-boat form, represents the ultimate in simplicity, in both setting up and handling. It is a supremely reliable rig as it has no metal fittings, no standing rigging, and only two or three pieces of running rigging (sheet, snotter and halyard, if rigged). It also sets a larger area of sail on a shorter mast than any other rig. Although the sprit rig is best suited to small craft under about 20ft overall, it is frequently used as an auxiliary sail on rowing boats, where it causes a minimum of interference with the primary functions of the boat, whether rowing or fishing, or used as a tender, etc. Thanks to the short length of the spars, the entire rig can be brailed up and unshipped in a few moments, and laid in the boat, well off to one side and out of the way.

A sail like this gave me my first experience with the sprit rig, when I was given the job of fitting out a rather fine-lined rowing tender to sail. Just previously, I had been sailing an International Moth, whose fully battened sail was a superb example of aerodynamic efficiency, but which made the boat more difficult to sail – and to keep from capsizing – than any other boat/rig combination I had experienced (or ever expect to). But having worked with and appreciated the performance of that sail, I thought the spritsail rig looked rather primitive and strange, and highly suspect from the point of view of aerodynamic efficiency.

But I set her up the way I'd seen it done, and was duly amazed to find out how well it functioned. It was all so easy! Put the mast through the hole, set up a line or two, and you're sailing. We weren't likely to embarrass any Moths, but the little boat moved out quite capably to windward, all under control, and I had to admit that sitting around comfortably in the boat made an interesting change from hanging out over the side in sheets of spray. I was learning the true significance of a low centre of effort. The sail's shape didn't look too good when the sprit was on the lee of it, but there seemed to be little difference in performance from one tack to the other. In fact, the sprit distorted the sail a lot less than I had expected. [...]

The basic arrangement involves a four-sided, generally loose-footed sail whose peak is outstretched by a sprit and rigged to the mast by means of a snotter. The peak of the sail is usually fitted with a rope becket, which fits over the tapered end of the sprit, and can thus be released instantly when the snotter is cast off and the tension eased. This snotter (an unattractive word, to say the least, but that's what it's called) is what makes the whole thing work. As it is hauled on, it forces the sprit up and outward to position the peak and set the sail. This snotter must be strongly rigged and reliable, because if it lets go under pressure, the sprit could come down hard enough to cause some damage. [...]

Snotters are generally belayed at the heel of the sprit, or to the mast. However, especially on a light boat, it can be safer and more convenient to lead the hauling part aft, where it can be reached more easily. Although synthetic materials don't generally offer great advantages in these traditional rigs, pre-stretched Dacron line could be a good choice for a snotter, which is prone to stretching and often needs frequent adjustment according to the wind strength and direction. A cam cleat could make snotter adjustment even easier. [...]

The thumb cleat, which supports the snotter, preventing it from sliding down the mast, may be positioned by trial and error. A second, lower cleat may be used for reefing. Basically, the idea is to set the sprit quite low on the mast so as to give the sprit more leverage against the head of the sail. If the sprit is too high, the angle between it and the sail's head becomes too fine, and excessive tension is needed to peak up the sail, which in turn puts a lot of extra stress on both the masthead and sprit. Conversely, if the sprit is carried too low on the mast, it can put limitations on reefing, as well as making the sprit longer than it needs to be. (Small-boat sprits are usually about as long as the mast, both being a little shorter than the boat's overall length.)

chapter 7

BACK TO THE ROOTS

'IN JAPAN, WHEN AN APPRENTICE potter is learning to turn a bowl, the master potter takes whatever the apprentice makes, throws it against the wall and makes him start again. The idea is to force him to lose his ego and learn the essence of making the perfect bowl. The individual bowls themselves don't matter, it's the learning that matters.'

As apocryphal stories go, this one, told by Iain one blustery afternoon at his workshop in Findhorn, pretty well sums up what he had to go through before tackling his next project. It all started simply enough, with Anton Fitzpatrick (who had organized the boatbuilding 'masterclass' with Iain the year before) asking him to scale up the lines of a model faering which he wanted to build full size. Iain took one look at the drawings and gently suggested that he could probably do better – in fact, he describes the drawings Anton sent him as 'decadent', implying they strayed so far from the original as to become a pastiche.

But a faering is a very particular boat; a double-ended workhorse used by fishermen on the coast of Norway for all purposes and in all weathers, it has a near mythical status in the seafaring world. And 'designing' – perhaps 'reinterpreting' would be a better word – a boat that's evolved over hundreds of years and which generations of boatbuilders have fine-tuned to perfectly fulfil its function isn't something you take on lightly. It's the nautical equivalent of redesigning the Parthenon or rewriting the Bhagavad Gita.

Iain had admired the type ever since he had first seen them while touring Norway in the 1970s. Indeed, it was the sight of these minimal craft drawn up on the beach or rowing across a fjord that had, in part, convinced him that he should become a boat designer. 'Wandering around in Norway, the old VW bus would frequently drop anchor and bring up suddenly as a wee boat hove in sight,' he later wrote. 'Some were in daily use; others were mouldering away on the shore of the fjord. But all fascinated me with their elegance of line; they seemed to be a supreme example of functional simplicity, an artefact perfectly suited to its purpose.'

A quarter of a decade later, he returned to that original inspiration to find the 'essence' of the design for himself. But, as he points out in his design catalogue, these boats weren't ever designed in the first place: they were shaped 'by hand and eye' without the benefit of drawings, patterns or moulds. Despite the apparent simplicity of the type, committing the shape to paper was, he wrote, a daunting task. 'Building this way is a highly refined art form, derived from generations of experience; is it not a little presumptuous to attempt to design a new boat which would look convincing on the Hardanger Fjord? The parameters seemed

Iain's inspiration for the Elf design came from the faerings he had admired in Norway 25 years earlier. (Photo: Iain Oughtred.)

somehow subtly different to my usual criteria – will it work, will it look good, can it be built easily? This one had to look right to folk who had grown up with these boats.'

As for building the boat in plywood, he defended the approach, saying: 'It may seem sacrilegious to build such a venerable type in plywood; however, some traditional craft are being planked in ply in Norway. As well as practical considerations, there is the difficulty of finding good planking stock of top quality larch or Norway spruce in widths over 12in. A plywood boat can be made to look traditional...'

Once again, Iain set about the task in his usual methodical manner, studying every photo and every design drawing he could find, and comparing the characteristics of the different craft. It soon became clear that no two faerings were exactly alike. What's more, because the brief was for a smaller boat than the traditional vessels of this type and because it was intended to fulfil such a different purpose (ie as a pleasure boat rather than a beast of burden), there was no single boat that Iain could base his design on. So, after consulting all the reference material, he took a deep breath and started drawing his own, 'Oughtred', faering.

Although traditionally every faering builder developed his own particular hull shape to suit the local conditions, generally speaking, the boats from Norway's west coast tended to have a narrower waterline beam, slacker bilges and more flare than the firmer-bilged boats from the fjords. Iain's design tended towards the latter, although it was shorter and fatter than most boats of this type. Typically of the type, both ends were fine below the waterline, but gained buoyancy dramatically above the waterline – as Iain said, the boat was not intended to brutishly take the 'hammering of the seas' but to 'lightly skim the surface, floating like a seabird'.

As it was to be built in plywood instead of solid timber, many of the details of the hull construction had to be adapted to the new medium. The boat retained the distinctive inclined frames (or rongs) at the stem and stern, but gained a small pair of breasthooks; light, laminated frames replaced the heavy traditional frames held together with trenails; the keel was made in two parts to save

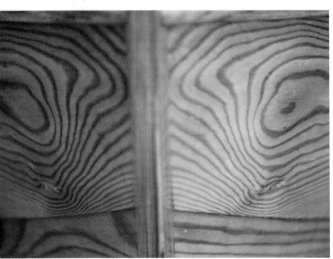

TOP Mairead's sprit rig may not be the most efficient, but it certainly looks the part. (Photo: Kathy Mansfield.)

ABOVE The boat was built using sustainable timber, including expensive larch plywood from Germany. (Photo: Kathy Mansfield.)

cutting into a large baulk of timber; and the thwarts were glued in place rather than slotting loosely into their supports. The Elf – as the design was named, after a mythical Viking water sprite – was offered with a daggerboard and a simple sprit rig.

The result was a boat that was much more traditional than Iain's previous designs, with a simple, restrained elegance – a shape as classic and timeless as a Japanese bowl. Through a process of refinement and paring things down, he had arrived at his own 'essential' boat, and this time it was much less about him than about the boat itself. 'It was the first time,' he says, 'I tried to completely let go of putting myself into a design.'

Although Anton built the prototype Elf at his workshop in Devon (lowering the sheer by an inch in the process), Iain was never completely happy with the outcome and soon after decided to build the boat for himself. With the environmental movement now finally gathering pace, several decades after Iain and the other pioneers of the wooden boat movement had argued for a more sustainable approach towards boatbuilding, Iain decided to make the boat as far as possible out of sustainable timber. *Classic Boat* magazine had already built its 14ft Port Isaac Lugger entirely out of FSC-certified timber, but apart from that the marine trade in Britain seemed to be remarkably slow at responding to the 'green wave' sweeping the country. Just sourcing the timber would prove problematic.

'I spoke to the people at Bruynzeel and asked them where their gaboon comes from. They told me in great detail how tightly controlled the cultivation of their timber is and how all the trees they use have to be replaced, otherwise they would go out of business. But they kept ominously quiet about mahogany and just said that, as far as they knew, all their woods are sustainably sourced.'

Eventually, Iain heard of some larch plywood being manufactured by a company in Germany and clubbed together with two other boatbuilders – Gorch von Blomberg from Hamburg and Frank Schofield in Norfolk – to order a batch of 40 sheets between them. By the time transport costs to Britain were factored in, the wood worked out at about £140 per sheet, or about twice the price of Bruynzeel. The solid timber for the boat was almost all local oak and larch, while the pine for the spars came from a timber yard at Inverness. For the oars, Iain used the staves of an old whisky barrel discarded from a local distillery, which gave off a wonderfully potent smell as he sawed them into shape.

Iain named his boat *Mairead* and finished her completely in oil – the better to show off her expensive larch plywood planking.

The essential boat. Mairead looks every bit the work of art she is, moored on a beach in Findhorn Bay. (Photo: Iain Oughtred.)

For nearly a year after she was launched, he rowed her around Findhorn Bay before he could finally bring himself to cut a slot in the bottom for the daggerboard and fit the rig. He was particularly intrigued by her performance in the steep waves thrown up by the sand bar at the harbour entrance, and almost caused himself an injury one day when the bow suddenly dropped into the trough of a particularly large wave and he found himself falling through thin air. He didn't break any bones on that occasion, but the forward thwart still bears the scar of his landing. Despite this, his description of the boat's rowing performance was described by *WoodenBoat* as 'just this side of ecstatic' when he told them: 'She handles well in seriously rough water. I've had her in steep, tall waves where few boats her size could live. She tracks extraordinarily well.'

Iain's days of surfing his faering were brought to an abrupt end when, in December 2000, he fell off a ladder at his workshop in Findhorn and cracked his skull on the concrete floor. There was no particular reason for him to fall, although he had been suffering from a bout of asthma and was feeling a bit 'woozy' from standing up too suddenly. Whatever the cause, the next thing he knew was that he was lying on his back on the floor, vaguely aware of people 'hovering about' him and eventually being rushed to hospital in an ambulance.

He spent Christmas 2000 in hospital in Elgin and, for the first time in many years, got to see Father Christmas. Apart from that, however, hospital bored him and, despite having a fractured skull and shoulder, he checked himself out within a week. Luckily he was sharing a house with the kindly Susanna, who took it upon herself to cook him health-giving soups to help restore his shattered body. It took him rather longer to recover his full health, however, and for the next few months he was pretty much an invalid. He lost a lot of weight, too, dipping from his already lean 10 stones to a decidedly frail 8½ stone. It took at least 18 months before he fully recovered.

To add to his woes, three weeks after leaving hospital, he was threatened with eviction from his workshop, where he was halfway through building his latest design, a scaled-down, round-bilged version of the Ness Yawl. Soon after moving into the building, Iain had bought a wooden garden shed which he placed in his space to use as an office/studio. It looked slightly eccentric, but it gave him a self-enclosed space to do his design work away from the noise and dust of the workshop. Now, the carpenter he sublet the space from decided he needed the space and gave him an ultimatum: either move the shed out by the end of the month, or move everything out (including a half-built boat) by the end of the following month. The timing could hardly have been worse, but with the help of a few friends Iain managed to get the shed shifted. It was only a matter of time, he realized, before he would have to move out completely.

The summer before, he had been to a music workshop on the Isle of Skye and had been captivated by the place in the same way he had been on his first visit there with Mouse all those years before, during his visit to Scotland in 1966. Now, Skye had a thriving artistic and musical scene and, although it was even more isolated than Findhorn, Iain sensed that there was a community he would be able to fit in with. The island even had its own magazine, *Skye Views*, which fostered the impression of an area bustling with cultural activity.

When the moment finally came for him to move out of his workshop – this time with four weeks' notice – he decided the time had come to finally make the long-awaited move. Only this time he decided to try to buy a place of his own, so that he wasn't continually at the mercy of other people's good intentions. Aged 61, he was finally ready to 'drop the anchor' and settle down in one place – for a while at least. Jo Fox, the founder of *Skye Views*, offered to put him up for a week while he looked for a place to live, and his friend Susanna volunteered to accompany him. She too could only spare a week, however, and when after six days of searching they hadn't found anything, Iain's future started to look a little precarious.

On the last day, just as they were about to give up, they stopped for lunch at the An Tuireann Arts Centre in Portree. Iain got chatting to a bladesmith who was exhibiting there, who told them a friend of his was selling a small house just up the road. The property, it turned out, was a derelict cottage eight miles west of Portree. It was small and extremely basic and about as isolated as you could get without going to one of the outer islands. But it was surrounded by some of the most dramatic scenery in the British Isles and came with enough land to build a studio and a workshop on, when time and finances allowed. Best of all, it cost just £25,000 – a fraction of the price of a similar property on the mainland, never mind further south.

Two weeks later, Iain came back and, with the help of a couple of local carpenters, started making the place habitable. They built a kitchen, insulated the roof and made a new porch. Then came the interesting bit. A few years before, Iain and some friends had concocted a plan to build three houses on a plot of land at Findhorn. Iain had even gone as far as having a studio made for himself. Some 21ft long by 11ft wide, it was built by Sveinung to Iain's design, and, with its lapstrake sides and chunky curved windows, looked like a cross between a boathouse and a goblin's cottage. Although the house building project never happened, after buying his cottage, Iain had it transported to Portree. Once there, it took a further two weeks of work with a JCB (a mechanical digger) and a chain hoist, before it could finally be inched over railway sleepers into place. Tucked under the trees at the front of the cottage, it made a picturesque sight, although it was too cold to use as a studio and soon turned into a workshop instead.

Meanwhile, he had found a temporary berth for his faering *Mairead* as an exhibit at the An Tuireann Arts Centre – not the first time a boat has been recognized as an art object, but surely one of the most deserving. She would end up finding a more permanent home with boatbuilder Jamie Clay and his wife Tessa, based on the Blackwater River in Essex.

Twixt land and sea. Iain found a new home among the burgeoning artistic community on the Isle of Skye. (Photo: John McPherson.)

Long before Struan Cottage was properly habitable, Iain was back at the drawing board, reworking some old designs. From designing and building a 'green' plywood faering such as Elf, it was a short step to designing one for solid timber construction. For, despite the difficulty of sourcing good planking timber, the most environmentally friendly form of boatbuilding must be, as it's always been, traditional plank on frame construction using real chunks of timber from sustainably managed sources. No need to use up the world's scarce oil resources to make glue, and after a century or two, when the boat is no longer needed, it can feed a good fire or just rot away into the ground from whence it came.

Sure enough, the order came from Colin Galloway, a retired hospital specialist who had caught the boatbuilding bug while taking part in Iain's masterclass with Anton. After building a couple of Iain's designs in plywood, he decided to try his hand at traditional construction and asked Iain for plans for a facring. It was a big leap to go from building epoxy ply dinghies to a solid timber faering, however, and Iain initially tried to put him off the idea. Colin was having none of it.

'I was taken with the type's elegant shape and apparent economy of construction,' he later wrote. 'As with so many traditional boats, faerings were built by eye and the skill passed down from father to son. Rather than being formed by moulds, planks were shored up from the floor and down from an overhead beam; their positions were determined by a few basic measurements – by builders of long experience. If I were to build an Oselver, I would have to adapt the construction to my skill level… In building the boat, it was my intention to try to keep broadly to a traditional form of construction insofar as this was possible. However, I cut many corners because of my total lack of traditional skills – as well as for convenience.'

The prototype Galloway Faering, as the design became known, was built of Scottish larch on seasoned oak, with traditional metal breasthooks (albeit made of stainless steel instead of wrought iron), loosely-fitted thwarts and wooden kabes in place of bronze rowlocks. Her planks were, however, sealed with marine mastic, rather than the more traditional mixture of horse's hair and tar.

The Scandinavian theme was soon taken up with another order for another traditionally-built boat, this time from former journalist-turned-boatbuilder Adrian Morgan. After years working on yachting magazines in London, Adrian had upped sticks and moved to Ullapool in Scotland, where he set up building boats the traditional way – in solid timber. His client, Roland Harris, an industrial archaeologist from Sussex, wanted a 'faering style' boat to be used on the East Coast rivers to teach his children to row and sail. The original idea was simply to adapt the Elf design for traditional construction, but once Iain got started on the design he got, as he put it, 'a little carried away' and ended up drawing a whole new set of plans. In fact, he had a perfect excuse to get carried away this time, as this boat was to be his 100th design.

'As the builder of Iain's 100th design, the responsibility hung heavy,' Adrian later wrote in *Classic Boat*. 'From the start it was made clear that any idea the client may have had for a "faering style" boat would not do. The boat had to be a faering or nothing, so any suggestion of more strakes than three was soon rejected in Iain's quiet but insistent way, and a laminated stem and stern – as opposed to solid, scarphed oak – didn't stand a chance.'

When Adrian received the plans for the Woodfish a few weeks later, he was astonished at the amount of detail they contained, to the extent that 'every rivet was depicted, not as a circle, but as a dot within a circle – with allowance made for perspective'. It's likely that Iain did get

Iain stands by the transplanted studio and his latest design, Jeanie II, outside his cottage in Skye. (Photo: courtesy Iain Oughtred.)

a little too 'carried away' and perhaps did lavish a bit more attention than usual on this symbolic set of plans, but generally his plans are well-known for their careful attention to detail; a feature of his work that had become a major selling point with amateur designers grateful for every bit of guidance they can get. Like Fabian Bush two decades before, however, Adrian riled against such control-freakery.

'Iain can be accused of over-designing,' he wrote. 'His response is that he produces plans for Everyman, and that means defining everything to achieve a result that pleases the owner and does not disgrace the designer. He wants every boat he draws to be built as drawn; anything less, you sense, pains his eye. For plywood/epoxy construction, that is achievable; less so in solid timber. Plywood is inert, dead; it goes where it is told. Timber has a life of its own...'

The issue came to a head over the boat's 'horns', the extensions of the fore and aft stems that stick up above the gunwales and give the faerings a great deal of their character. Adrian had apparently suggested, to Iain's horror, making the aft 'horn' removable to allow a conventional tiller to be fitted instead of the 'push-pull' arrangement specified in the plans. Iain managed to talk him out of that idea, but couldn't stop other subtle alterations.

'Iain has clear ideas about the shape of his stems and sterns, and the shape of the horns was defined precisely,' wrote Adrian. 'My excuse [for changing the shape] was simple: if a builder cannot add something of his personality to his boat, then it is merely building by numbers. A traditional faering is organic, and her shape changes by the day. . . To build as close as possible to Iain's plans was one thing; to reproduce slavishly every detail, was another, so Iain's Woodfish has my horns (and a few other subtle features that only we would know about).'

Adrian's article gives other insights into the difficulties of collaborating with a perfectionist designer: 'Working with Iain was a privilege only occasionally tinged with frustration at the lengths to which he would go, even during the building process, to refine and modify. A day or so after the curved cross pieces [i.e. beams] had been laminated... an envelope arrived from Struan Cottage. A modification that only after placing the new sheet over the old elicited any difference – a difference of ⅜in (9.5mm) in the thickness of the cross member, and a difference that would have made no difference in strength. Iain's modification did, however, look a wee bit more elegant and was a smidgen lighter...'

By way of an answer, and to prove that he is not the control freak sometimes portrayed, Iain described 'the roughest boat ever built to one of [his] designs'. It was a Seahorse Skiff which a friend

The Woodfish was Iain's 100th design and was built for an industrial archeologist from Sussex. (Photo: courtesy Iain Oughtred.)

of his slapped together in a matter of weeks while going through various life traumas. The friend launched the boat without paint or varnish, and little fountains of water appeared in the bottom where the nail holes hadn't been filled properly. His solution was to take a box of matches along whenever he went sailing and plug the leaks with matches. Eventually, he slapped some varnish on the boat and used her for several years, including six months neglected on a beach in Spain, before belt-sanding and repainting her. Iain uses the story to demonstrate the superiority of wood over glassfibre, arguing that no glassfibre boat would have survived such abuse, as well as to suggest that fine craftsmanship isn't always necessary or appropriate. The roughly put together skiff was just what his friend needed at that point in his life and he, as designer, was more than happy for his design to be used in such a way.

Iain's commitment to buying sustainable timber, however, seems to have waned with time. 'A while ago this guy came from British Columbia and spoke about the destruction caused there by the logging, and I promised then I wouldn't buy Canadian wood. The trouble is, if you are going to build a boat, you need Sitka spruce for the spars and yellow pine for planks, and most of that comes from British Columbia. It's nice to be uncompromising and Green, but you have to limit yourself in the materials you use and the kinds of boats you can build. If I was totally uncompromising, I wouldn't be able to build a canoe out of plywood – or, if I build a traditional one, I wouldn't be able to use Alaskan yellow cedar, which is such beautiful stuff! If you are going to build boats, you have to compromise. Boatbuilding uses only a tiny fraction of the wood being felled, and the boats last such a long time.'

Ever the perfectionist, since the beginning Iain has had a tendency to revisit old designs and improve them. Even his hugely successful Acorn Skiff has been through a continual process of adjustment and refinement – not that it was always appreciated by his clients. Jamie Clay, who built six Acorns, remembers changes Iain made to the Mk2 and Mk3 versions, first filling out the bow a little and then decreasing the number of planks in the hull to make it easier to build. After speaking to him on the phone, Iain admitted that his changes wouldn't make a great deal of difference to the performance of the boat, and Jamie carried on building the old version. He already had his moulds cut out and the planking lines marked out and saw no reason to start over again.

For Iain, however, it's not just about building half a dozen boats but about creating a legacy that, even long after he has 'weighed anchor and headed off into the sunset', will be built by amateurs and professionals alike for decades and possibly centuries to come. To that end, in the late 1990s he started redrawing some of his favourite designs. It all started when he was asked to redraw the Caledonia Yawl for a client in Germany who wanted to build the boat with a 'round' bilge. This meant increasing the number of planks on each side from four to seven to 'smooth out' the angle between them, giving the boat a more traditional appearance and bringing it closer to the Shetland yoles which were its original inspiration.

While he was redrawing the design, Iain decided to tweak the lines to improve its sailing performance. And, once he had revamped the Caledonia Yawl, he couldn't resist doing the same with the rest of the double-enders. When he had first conceived the designs, he had imagined they would be used as much for rowing as for sailing and he had drawn them long and lean with that in mind. In practice, however, the boats were used far more under sail than oar. So he decided to broaden and firm up the bilge – effectively making the bottom flatter – to give them more stability. The more stability they had, the more sail they could carry and the better they would sail. In the process, the Ness Boat grew from 16ft 6in to 17ft and was renamed the Tirrik, while the Whilly Boat grew from 14ft 6in to 15ft and was renamed the Whilly Tern.

'I didn't make a lot of changes to the Caledonia Yawl,' he says. 'I refined the outline shape, the shape of the stem, worked on the layout of the interior, and added a bit more detail. The smaller ones, though, I totally redesigned. I took a very similar approach: I refined the lines, with taller, more elegant rigs. They all became fatter and more stable and should now have better sailing performance to windward. The plans are better and more professional now, easier to read and with quite a lot more detail.'

After the double-enders came the canoes. This time, Iain felt they had too many planks and needed too many moulds, too close together, to build. So he simplified the whole structure, adding a bit more flare on the way. And again, he couldn't resist including more of the pernickety detail which so infuriated Adrian but which proved so valuable for the amateur builder. His aim, he says, was to produce a more complete and usable set of plans which would be 'easier for the builder and more accurate as well'.

He then turned his attention to the rowing dinghies, starting with the Auk, from which he chopped about 1in off the freeboard because he thought it looked 'a bit exaggerated'. He then scaled the plans down to 91% to produce a 7ft version – the 'absolute minimum size' for a boat of this type – adding a couple of inches to the beam, as well as a little bit more flare, and widening the transom slightly to make the boat 'as capacious as possible'. When interviewed for this book, he was about to embark on an enlarged version of the Tammie Norrie, scaling it up from 13ft 6in to 16ft 5in.

It was a huge amount of work which, Iain freely admits, wasn't entirely appreciated by his potential customers, with several of his regular builders choosing to stick with the existing designs. But for Iain it was a question of professional pride.

'As long as I have the feeling that this thing's not quite right, I'm not content until I can tear it to bits and sort it out! With the canoes, I kept looking at the plan and thinking of refinements and changes I'd make if I was doing them again. The more I thought about that, the more unhappy I was every time I got an order for them. I would think, "Can't you wait a couple of months? I can give you something much better than this!" In 2006, I finally got around to redrawing them. Now, I really enjoy getting an order because I can pull out the plans and think, yeah, this guy's getting something really good.'

Two years after moving to Skye, Iain got a call from Robert Ayliffe, the then proprietor of Duck Flat Wooden Boats, an Australian company that runs a boatbuilding school, sells books and plans and generally does everything it can to get people on the water in beautiful wooden boats. Robert offered Iain a free ticket to attend the Wooden Boat Festival at Goolwa in South Australia. Tucked up snug and cosy in his cottage in Skye, the increasingly reclusive designer was reluctant to exchange the mist and cool of a Scottish winter for the blazing heat of an Australian summer. Robert was persuasive, however, and Iain wanted to support his cause – plus it was an opportunity to see his mother, who he hadn't seen for 24 years and was now quite ill.

Jeanie had been poorly for some time, and Iain had been feeling increasingly under self-imposed pressure to visit her. It was a problem he had brought to his Taizé prayer meeting one day and had had an overwhelming feeling that he didn't need to worry about it just yet, and that everything would be all right. It was the kind of 'message' or intuition he had had in the past, and he had learned to trust it. So he let things ride. This, however, was an opportunity he knew he shouldn't miss. He was also hoping to meet up with his son, Haig, who he hadn't seen since that meeting in London over 20 years ago – although, perhaps not surprisingly for such a fragmented family, no one seemed to know where he was.

Iain flew to Australia the 'long way', via Los Angeles, because he thought it would make the jetlag better and in order to visit his brother, who was living on a Cal 39 sloop in LA. His plans nearly came unstuck when he found himself stranded at the airport without enough money to pay for his onward flight and had to spend a stressful hour ringing his friends for help. He eventually made it to Sydney in time for Jeanie's 88th birthday and received the welcome due to a returning prodigal son. 'Her memory is out the window,' he later wrote, 'but she seems to find me unforgettable.'

Since the death of Iain's father, Jeanie had become increasingly interested in environmental matters and had sent Iain long letters discussing the state of the world and, particularly, the plight of endangered species. She joined Friends of the Earth, took part in their annual awareness day in Sydney Harbour, with their inflatable whale, and spent a great deal of time at her balcony watching the birds and enjoying the sunsets. 'As she grew older, she developed an innocent, childlike wonder at how beautiful everything really was, beneath all the crap that was going on.'

Being reunited with his mother wasn't the only emotional drama in store for Iain in Sydney. His brother Rick had managed to track Haig down and had invited him to come to Jeanie's birthday, along with his German wife and their two children. But if anyone was expecting an emotional meeting between Iain and the son he hadn't seen for about 15 years, they would have been disappointed. 'It wasn't a dramatic reunion,' Iain remembers. 'Haig came in and said hi, and we had a cup of tea and a biscuit. No one would have thought we didn't see each other every week.'

After a three-day journey on a paddle steamer down the Murray River, Iain was welcomed as a celebrity in Goolwa and treated as the guest of honour he undoubtedly was. According to the organizers, at least 30 of the 300 boats there were built to his designs, including two Grey Seals, three Eun na Maras and, most bizarrely, a decked-over Puffin fitted with a 9hp diesel and stabilizers. It was all a long way from his last visit to Australia as a struggling designer with half a dozen designs to his credit. He later wrote: 'Funny, in a way, after a meteoric career (meteoric meaning I think something that appears for a brief moment, burns out and disappears) building and racing the National Gwen 12s on Sydney Harbour up until 1964, to return and be famous for designing the kind of traditionally-inspired boats that hardly anyone would have taken notice of 39 years ago.'

Stranger still to fly half way round the world and to be more famous than on your own front doorstep. In an article for the Wooden Boat Builders Trade Association's quarterly journal *Soundings*, Iain described a meeting that summed up the special status he enjoyed – despite his best efforts to remain invisible. 'I was admiring one of the 10ft Puffin dinghies. The owner turned up, and I said she was one of the best I had seen. We chatted a while. He said: "I'm told Iain Oughtred is around here somewhere." I said: "Aye, he was here a minute ago; he's not far away." (Thinking this is a bit silly.) He said: "What's he wearing?" I said: "A baggy old pair of jeans, and a Duck Flat T-shirt." (Thinking this is getting really silly.) At last he says: "Oh, you're not...?"'

Back in Sydney, he spent more time with his mother and the rest of the family, including a sail on the bay on a boat his son (by now referred to as 'Haggis') owned a part-share in ('typical fat ugly 25ft state-of-the-art cruising yacht'). He revisited his old haunts in Middle Harbour, including the old Mosman Amateur Sailing Club shed which, miraculously, had been saved from the developer's diggers by a conservation order and was virtually unchanged. He mourned the loss of the elegant old ferries, but delighted at the development of the fairly outrageous skiffs, famed for their clouds of sail and edge-of-the-seat ride. He even found time to meet up with some of the old Gwen 12 sailors he hadn't seen since his racing days ('Great bunch of guys; good sailors. Surprising to find them looking older than they did 30 years ago.')

After four weeks in Australia, he flew back to Britain via Vancouver BC to visit his long-time mentor Paul Gartside (to see 'how a real professional boat designer works') and catch up with old girlfriend Katarina. He then stopped off at Port Townsend in Washington, otherwise known as 'Boat Heaven' for its concentration of boatbuilders, where he caught up with Kees Prins, who had taught boatbuilding in Holland and built several of Iain's boats back in the 1990s. He finished his 35,000-mile journey relieved to be home in Skye but once again wondering whether he shouldn't be working in a more stimulating and creative atmosphere.

Three months after he got home, his mother died. One last visit from the prodigal son was, it seemed, all she had desired. Iain wrote movingly of her last days: 'Jeanie O waited, just long enough, before quietly fading away. She went through the whole process gracefully, patiently, giving her kids plenty of time to get used to the idea. She was ready. She had not had an easy life, but always seemed grateful to be alive. What an achievement! – I think, to be so at peace with yourself, the world, everything, and to be totally ready when your time comes to move on. And that I was able to spend that little time with her seems almost miraculous. One or two people said, "Oh, I'm sorry." I think – nothing to be sorry about! She's fine.'

Reunited with his mother in Sydney after an absence of 24 years. She died soon afterwards. (Photo: courtesy Iain Oughtred.)

IAIN ON BOATBUILDING IN AUSTRALIA

(Extract from the *Wooden Boat Builder's Trade Association Quarterly*, Issue 28, Autumn 2003)

An interesting visit with Frank Bethwaite. He has of course had a tremendous influence on the development of small craft. And Julian likewise, in the skiff department. Frank's Tasars are still popular (though I think less attractive than the development-class NS 14s that they developed from). He is justly proud of his new 59er; I was interested to see this one, having thought that a grown-up version of the 29er would be just about ideal. But no trapeze – Frank doesn't seem to like trapezes, although it must be the most significant advance in racing-boat design since Uffa Fox's time. (Uffa wanted the trapeze, of course, and his boats needed it, but he wasn't allowed to do it.) Frank wants middle-aged women to feel able to crew the boat. I wonder if even some of them might prefer to sit back comfortably in a nice trapeze harness than break their backs sitting out. But there is no doubt the 59er is a highly refined and efficient little sailing machine, by a master of the art. (Or craft, rather; there's not much art in these things.)

The brilliant B14 appeared at the London Dinghy Exhibition in the early 1980s. In epoxy-sandwich construction it was about as light as a 1950s Gwen 12. It was regarded as being way ahead of its time, and it took a long time to begin to get established in Britain. One (arguable) improvement was a trapeze and narrower wings, but this was unfortunately scrapped in the interests of international racing.

Eventually British manufacturers began to try to get up to date, producing some real rubbish. The right sort of gear: asymmetric spinnaker, trapeze etc, but very heavy hulls, of the cheapest possible polyester fibreglass construction, and design and build quality far inferior to the Australian boats. What had been our favourite dinghy-racing magazine pushed these boats with undiscriminating enthusiasm, being blatantly more interested in advertising revenue than in encouraging good boats.

Dave Ovington is producing the Bethwaite boats in the north of England. But he now has some serious competition from Racing Sailboats, who are also building some impressive single- and two-handed boats, of almost comparable quality. A difficult business in a way: in a country which has been said to have almost more classes than boats, it is not easy to get a new one established. And the capital cost of setting up for production must be enormous. And it needs to be right first time. (Sometimes is. . .).

It is a very different scene now. Planning a new boat used to be a long term project, involving either lengthy discussions with the boatbuilder and months of waiting before the boat was ready for the owner to start fitting her out, according to his own requirements, or, of course, building her yourself. Either way, an intimate relationship with the boat had time to evolve and mature. The boat would be a significant event in one's life; always unique, always to be remembered.

Now it is all much more high tech, with something nearer to true one-design racing, along with a bland conformity. You buy the boat 'off the shelf', and it ('it') looks exactly the same as all the others. Which are less easily recognizable during a race. Confession: I've done it, with a half-share in a 29er, just for fun, and for the experience – not having the time to do it the old way. An excellent design; really a logical extension of the boats we were sailing in the 1960s. Needing minor refinements, like the installation of a mainsheet snatchblock, and the elimination of as many as possible of those wretched little ring-clips (which are difficult to fit with dry hands and practically impossible with cold wet hands. Is this an English aberration?).

A new development from America – of all places! – is a strip-planked wooden boat, by Bram Dally of Seattle. Called the Swift Solo, she looks much like a highly refined 29er – with more sail. He sails her single-handed, and seems to think normal people will be able to. Maybe Moth sailors. . .

An impressive achievement, and hopefully it may set some sort of a precedent. Wood boats can do it – better! But I think Bram's hopes of getting a class established may be thin, given the single-handed stipulation, and the very sophisticated construction. The materials cost is almost as much as a 29er. Plus 350-plus hours of skilled work. I would love to do a plywood two-handed boat. But are there still enough potential builders? Even working from a kit? Could it not be mass-produced economically? Who is going to try it?

As well as being home buildable/repairable, the wood boat will, of course, be more durable. A Merlin can remain competitive for ten years or more; some fibreglass boats (eg 470) are reputed to get too soft and floppy after two or three seasons' racing to be competitive.

This is how Consumerism works. They prefer to grab something cheap off the shelf than spend 10% or 25% more for a craftsman-built item of far superior quality that will last three times longer. It's the Ford Escort syndrome: a lot of these guys wouldn't be seen dead in an Escort, yet in buying a small boat they'll go for that quality – it looks all right when it's shiny and new and everyone else has got one, so it must be OK.

And the wood boats can, of course, look interestingly recognizable. Most of the new class boats look much the same. If they want to make one look distinctive and rakish, they increase the standard 20% off-vertical stem angle to 25%. Not for much longer will we see, in one- or two-of-a-kind races, the wonderful variety of unique designs: the Hornet, Albacore, FD, National 12, Finn, 10sq m canoe, 505, etc etc. Mostly British designs, of course; most still popular, or at least well known everywhere.

In epoxy-sandwich construction, the B14 was about as light as a Gwen12 (above). (Photo: Joy Falls.)

chapter 8

EPILOGUE

OPPOSITE *Iain rowing his faering* Mairead *through the surf during the author's first visit to Findhorn. (Photo: Nic Compton.)*

BELOW *Standing outside the controversial hut at his workshop in Findhorn. (Photo: Nic Compton.)*

IT'S A CLEAR DAY WHEN the plane touches down at Inverness. The sky immediately looks much bigger and the landscape more emphatic than further south – as if human habitation has a more perilous grip on the soil and might be swept away at any minute. It's colder too and, while I wait for my bus, I buy a fleece top and hat from a camping shop and shove them in my rucksack, just in case.

The road from Inverness to the Isle of Skye is a traveller's delight, crossing the heart of the country from the Moray Firth on the east coast to the legendary Western Isles. First there is the sinister gloom of Loch Ness, followed by the ragged majesty of Glen Moriston and Glen Shiel, with their intimidating skylines of 1,000m-high peaks. There are streams and waterfalls everywhere, miniature castles pop up around every other corner, and in one particularly idyllic valley there is a herd of stags, exaggeratedly poised as if they had walked straight out of a painting. And then we reach the sea. After the picturesque beauty of the mountains, the sublime vastness of the ocean hits me like a blow to the stomach. On either side, the land lines the water with a range of steep blue-grey hills, while the deep blue sea ahead is punctuated by the shadows of a few clearly-defined islands.

Iain meets me at the bus stop, looking much as he did last time I visited him, nine years before. Perhaps his mat of curly hair has a little more white in it, and perhaps his lean frame is thinner and more wiry than before. We shake hands and then give each other a brief hug. I am here on business, but we are friends too.

It is dusk (or 'uht', as Iain would have it) as we drive the eight miles to Bernisdale, and he starts telling me about one of his recent projects. It's a sharpie, one of those boxy double-enders native of New England, which he has reinterpreted for plywood construction. The owner, Alastair Bremner, gave him one of his very first commissions – a Swampscott-style dory which became the John Dory, design No 25 – back in the early 1980s. Alastair sailed the 18ft *Asphodel* all around the Isles of Scilly for nearly 25 years before deciding to upgrade to something bigger. And again he asked Iain to look towards the hardy workboats of the East Coast of America for inspiration.

Iain jumped at the chance. While he was doing his sabbatical at *WoodenBoat* magazine, back in 1986, he had stumbled across a whole cabinet of sharpies designed by Ralph Munroe and had devoured the Captain's correspondence on the subject. Despite their ungainly appearance, sharpies are astonishingly seaworthy and the letters contained countless stories of them surviving extreme conditions either by partly raising their centreboards and sliding away from the waves or raising

As far from his native Australia as he could get, Iain found a rustic home in a remote part of Scotland. (Photo: Nic Compton.)

them completely and skimming into sheltered waters on their shallow draught. Twenty years later, Iain revisited those sources, and the result was design No 87.

But Alastair chose Devon boatbuilder Adrian Noyes to build the boat and, while Adrian is a craftsman steeped in the traditions of solid timber construction, he seems to have missed the point of this essentially simple, almost modernist design. Iain tells me how, although the sharpie has a flat-bottomed hull ideally suited to being built upside down, Adrian insisted on building it the right way up. This meant he had to jack the boat up to fit first one layer of plywood on the bottom and then again for the second. And there were other changes, such as sweeping the coachroof up fore and aft, adding another layer of complexity to its construction, and fitting standing rigging to the main mast, something traditional sharpies never needed.

As he fusses about how his design has been adulterated, I realize how long it is since we last met. When I visited Iain in Findhorn, he had just finished building his faering *Mairead* and was still rowing her, hesitating before he cut into her hull and added a centreboard for sailing. Since then, he has embarked on a whole new design path, bolder than much of what he's done before – the design notes of the sharpie even talk about carbon fibre masts, and she's hardly the conventionally pretty boat I've come to expect to spring from Iain's drawing board. Yet it's a natural evolution of his work so far, more so than previous cruising designs such as the Farne Islander, which seemed to appear out of nowhere and had no discernible Oughtred character, and serves as a reminder of how unwise it is to try to pigeon-hole him.

It's dark by the time we arrive at the cottage. The rooms are dimly lit, and the stone walls catch shadows, giving a gloomy air. The two rooms serve as both office and living areas: the kitchen has a small wooden table in the middle and a large drawing table by the window, while the living room is partly filled with two photocopiers (including an extra long one for the plans) and boxes of paper. Iain's bedroom is through a curtain in the middle of the house, while the guest room is a converted lean-to off the living room. The house is ascetically simple, if not to say spartan, and there are precious few home comforts, apart from a washing machine. On the shelves are boxes of cassettes, meticulously labelled by category ('Folk', 'Celtic', 'Classical', etc.) while the spare room is full of books showing his eclectic reading taste, from self-help manuals to books about philosophy, the history of Scotland, and poetry. Several half-models grace the walls, including a clipper-bowed cruising yacht which he designed early in his career, and shows clear influence of L Francis Herreshoff.

Outside, the boatshed looks perfectly at home, nestled in the trees, as if it has always been there, despite the two-week struggle to get into position. Inside, there are the basics of a simple workshop, with a bandsaw and a few hand tools. Occupying most of the floor space are the moulds and battens for his latest project, a 10ft 8in Stickleback canoe. Two scale models are lying on the bench: one of a Tumlare sloop, a favourite design of his, and the other of his own sharpie.

Parked in front of the shed are two boats on trailers: the prototype Arctic Tern *Jeanie II* and the Ness Yawl *Alba*, which he recently bought back from her original owner Charles-Henri and renamed *Albannach*. Both boats, I later discover, are for sale. Having tried them out in all manner of conditions and learned all their foibles, Iain is ready to move on and pass them on to someone else. He's always been like this. It's as if he's only really interested in sailing a boat while there's still a puzzle to solve and, once he's solved it, he loses interest. I wonder idly if there's a parallel in his relationships with women, but don't have the audacity to ask.

After a quick tour of the cottage, we sit down in the kitchen. Iain has made a vegetarian stew with great chunks of vegetables in it, which he dishes up and picks at judiciously, while I wolf mine down greedily, eating twice as much as he does. We open the red wine I've brought, and he sips modestly at his half glass, while I soon guzzle half a bottle. He speaks quietly about how he came across the cottage and about spending days moving the boatshed into position; I blather on about my new flat and the difficulties of juggling multiple responsibilities.

While I stay there, we each eat and drink from one bowl and one cup, and use one set of cutlery. Like Iain, I strip-wash at the sink and pee in the garden. Although, at just over 6ft tall, I am about the same height as Iain, I consistently eat about twice as much as he does and drink twice as much, too. At home, I am regarded as an introspective anti-consumer; here I feel like a loud-mouthed glutton.

And there's the cold. In fact, it's not much warmer inside than it is outside and, at the tail end of a Scottish winter, that's not very warm. To save on his oil bill, Iain rarely puts the central heating on, and the woodburning stove is in bits in the living room because the fumes give him asthma. I see that he is wearing six layers: a vest, a shirt, two fleeces, a jumper and a fleece shirt. My impromptu purchases at Inverness are immediately put to good use, but even they are not enough and, two days later, I admit defeat and borrow a pair of long johns from Iain.

It's not just boats! Iain plays several musical instruments and sings traditional Scottish songs. (Photo: Nic Compton.)

Iain's needs are minimal and he has exactly what he needs to eat, sleep and stay warm – no more and, just occasionally (it seems to me), a little less. It's as if he's measured what his bodily requirements are and is determined not to consume an iota more than he needs, and that includes food, warmth, space and, arguably, love. It's a skill learned from years living on the breadline and devoting himself to artistic and intellectual pursuits, when there was little leeway for self-indulgence. And of course it comes from his spiritual beliefs: from the Presbyterian regime enforced by his father, through to the earthly release of transcendental meditation, and the simple sobriety of his Quaker faith.

For three days, Iain talks about his life, either standing at the drawing table perched on one leg, or sitting at the table with his hands cupped around a mug of tea. He drinks green tea loose in the mug, and tops up the same dregs repeatedly, occasionally refreshing them with a new pinch of leaves.

His Scottish accent is more pronounced than it was last time I saw him and, whereas his words often acquired an Australian lilt when he was in full flow, this time I can hardly detect it at all. As ever, the conversation is punctuated by long pauses, while he collects his thoughts and words, during which it's hard to resist the temptation to prompt him with more questions. Later, when I listen to the recordings, I am struck by how my questions become fewer, the silences longer and his answers more in-depth, as I adjust myself to his pace. I also notice that, whenever he is uncomfortable with the line of questioning, his asthma miraculously returns and his replies are broken up by a whispery cough.

He talks about his early life with enthusiasm and great honesty: his domineering father, his tolerant, wise mother, his own social inadequacies and his difficulties with women. He remembers in astonishing detail the races he competed in half a century ago and recounts them, tack by tack, with details of the technical advantage of each boat he sailed.

Yet he talks reluctantly about his own design process and what makes his designs tick. He avoids analysing his designs and rarely mentions technical matters such as wetted surface area, coefficients and angles of heel. Like most artists, it seems, he's more comfortable creating and practising his art than talking about it. After all, his work is by definition an intuitive, aesthetic process, not easily put into words. Yet, when I start my research in earnest and unearth articles he wrote even 30 years ago, I find he is a fine writer, with a sensitive ear and a light, playful way with words.

There's a moment of insight when we talk about his Beaver design, a 16ft Canadian canoe commissioned by McNulty's Boats to be built in strip-plank. How does he go about designing something as quintessential as a canoe, I ask, when surely every type of canoe has already been produced? How can he find anything new to say about it? 'With a Canadian canoe, I don't want to bring anything new to it,' he answers, 'I just want to get it right, to get it as it should be, to make the archetypal Canadian canoe. All variations and designs are evolving towards the perfect canoe, and that's what I'm trying to achieve.'

Iain at the drawing board in his design hut in Findhorn. (Photo: Nic Compton.)

He then pulls out a book of canoe designs and flicks through the pages, pointing out the different shapes, how one is too rounded in the ends, another too flat; one has too much sheer, another too little. I'm astonished at the amount of variation between what initially seems like a single design. Bit by bit, I see what he is getting at, and I see that there really isn't a perfect canoe. I realize that the boat he has drawn really does seem to incorporate all the best features of the boats he has shown me, whilst at the same time having its own individual identity.

Again, I am struck by what an intuitive process designing these boats is. Perhaps if we were talking about modern racing boats, it would be easy to explain why this boat is shaped in such and such a way, and how this affects her performance. But asking Iain to talk about his work in this way goes against everything he and his boats stand for; trying to apply a technical approach to an intensely aesthetic philosophy. Not that his work won't stand up to rigorous scientific scrutiny, but it's not what the boats are about, and if that is your criteria, then you are missing the point.

He talks of his plans for the future as if he were a young man with most of his life ahead of him, rather than the 68-year-old he really is. There are still boats he'd like to design – nothing grand, just a few small cruising boats and a training dinghy for kids, like an updated Mirror, which he thinks is long overdue for a revamp. He'd also like to write a book on building a modern canoe using clinker plywood construction (glue-lap-ply in America). But it's not all just about boats. He's still keen to do other things, like writing and singing workshops, model making and photography.

His tireless curiosity keeps him young. Even at the start of the wooden boat revival back in the 1980s, Fabian Bush said he looked much younger than his early 40s. When I first met him, I assumed he was in his mid-40s not his mid-50s, and it's hard to believe he is now well past the age of retirement.

Yet he talks often of regrets: of his struggle to find his path in life, of places he left too soon, of women he was too hesitant to love. Visiting him in his isolated cottage, about as far from his native Sydney as he could possibly crawl, living alone in almost primitive conditions and still toiling tirelessly at his drawings, it's not how you would expect one of the most successful practitioners of their field to live. By rights, he should have a dedicated design studio, with assistants helping him draught his plans while he dreams up new ideas. He should have a workshop, with all the tools and materials to build prototypes of his designs. He should be living in a thriving creative community, that inspires him with artistic ideas and stimulating intellectual discussion. And he should have a family, with children tripping down the path to try out his latest creations.

Preparing Mairead *for an outing. The oiled finish shows off her expensive larch plywood planking to good effect. (Photo: Nic Compton.)*

There's no doubt his design career has been a long, hard struggle. It took eight years before he started earning more than £1 per hour, and it was only following the publication of his *Clinker Plywood Boatbuilding Manual* in 1998 that he started earning anything approaching the national minimum wage. Now, 27 years since he advertised his first set of dory plans in *PBO*, he has some 106 designs to his name, 36 of which are in his catalogue. Orders for his plans come from around the world – from about 60 countries at the last count, including Brazil, Colombia, Guadeloupe, Fiji, Papua New Guinea, the Solomon Islands, Bahrain, Oman, Mauritius, Japan, Zimbabwe… the list goes on. He currently sells about four plans a week and, whereas six years ago only 40% of those went overseas, that figure is now nearer 70%. *WoodenBoat* sells many times more.

He pulls out an old A5 notebook (half-size in the US) in which every sale he has ever made is recorded, in meticulous longhand. At the back, there are hand-drawn graphs comparing sales of his plans, suggesting Iain isn't as impervious to public opinion as first appears. His Guillemot design is the most popular, with 213 sales since 1991, closely followed by the Tammie Norrie, with 208 sales: both are very traditional, mid-range rowing/sailing boats with broad appeal. The Caledonia Yawl is selling better than usual because of an article in *WoodenBoat*, he tells me, while the diminutive Auk has received a boost from an article in *Classic Boat*. He himself doesn't sell many dories and canoes any more, but they are still popular in the USA.

It may not be the workshop/studio/family he dreamed of, but it is nevertheless an impressive legacy, and it is one that will undoubtedly survive for generations to come. For what raises Iain above the level of all his contemporaries – and what is the mark of his genius – is his ability to create designs that are at once timeless and 'classic', in the best sense of the word, and yet distinctly bear the seal of his own character and ethos. By truly entering the soul of his designs (not just the wetted surface area, coefficients and angles of heel), he produces craft of such complete integrity that they do become timeless and, in their way, perfect. And that is a formidable legacy to bequeath to the world.

Suddenly, the four days are up and Iain is driving me back to the bus stop. In a strangely circular way, he is talking again about the sharpie (and this time I have my dictaphone switched on). Having admired the functional beauty of the model in the workshop, I can now sympathize with Iain's point of view. By comparison, the boat that Adrian Noyes built looks fussy and 'yachty', as if it has lost touch with its working boat roots. As we approach Portree, there's time for one more question, and I ask the question that's been on the tip of my tongue for the last two days: have his relationships with women improved?

'Yes, but it was a long, long, long process of opening up and getting away from my little autistic, asthmatic childhood and my consequent inability to communicate. I had an interesting experience when I first got involved with the Quakers. I was at a big annual meeting, chatting to folk in a light superficial kind of way, and that evening I had a strong sense of how inadequate that was and a total failure to really reach people, or touch people, or really be with people. As if this meeting was the beginning of a process of sharing, and I was immediately stopping it in the first stages and going away.

'I've been thinking about that experience lately and thinking that, whoever you meet, it might be the bus driver or a guy in the post office or whatever, there's a potential contact to share things with, which can be useful in all sorts of unforeseen and unimagined ways. You need to be there and be aware of who this human is – it might be the only contact you ever have with them and your meeting might be useful somehow. You need to initiate that process and enable it to continue to wherever it should go, whether that's with people in general or establishing relationships with women.'

Back home, I contact Iain's brother David and sister Elizabeth in Australia. David, like Iain, emigrated from Australia in his early 20s and went to live in America for many years. Unlike Iain, he returned to Australia and now lives in Sydney. He is a keen and perceptive writer and describes the young Outhreds'/Oughtreds' upbringing in fascinating detail – his emails soon add up to nearly 4,000 words. He seems admiring of his older brother, although he confesses that Iain remains 'somewhat of a mystery'. He describes both his parents as 'dysfunctional' and, although he reserves most of his vitriol for his father, he holds them both responsible for Iain's inability to assimilate into Australian life.

'Under more salutary family circumstances, with greater social skills Iain may well have felt more integrated into society, become a family man, and developed a profitable business around his skills as a boatbuilder and designer, or possibly something else entirely. He probably would have stayed in Australia as a result.' And he concludes: 'On the positive side, particularly since Jean's passing, the siblings are developing a special bond because of what we went through together. We are beginning to appreciate the difficulties each of us faced, which led to the choices we made. I fervently hope we can all help each other to heal. It would be great for us if Iain would come back here.'

Elizabeth is more conciliatory. She too refers to the 'family dysfunction' but also points to the wonderful 'aesthetic environment' provided by their mother, the charm and humour of their father and the freedom they were given to roam around Sydney, which fostered her lifelong love of the city. She too seems pained by Iain's disappearance to the other side of the world. 'David

Iain rowed Mairead *for a full year before finally fitting her with a centreboard, tiller and mast for sailing. (Photo: Nic Compton.)*

has done much to confront his demons, and Iain has retreated into his magical mystery life of creativity in the gloomier climes of Scotland,' she writes. 'A greater contrast to the bright sunshine and colours of Australia one could never find!'

Iain, too, is defensive of his parents, especially his mother, and reminds me of the words she once wrote to him – words which show great self-awareness and which all parents would surely do well to ponder: 'I hope for understanding and forgiveness for our ignorance in trying to pass on the values we thought we were supposed to live by.' He sends me copies of her letters which, he says, shows her insight into the world, although I am most struck by the gentle, compassionate insight the letters reveal into her own son. There are observations about materialism, Aboriginal culture and nature, and then this:

'A happy birthday, my dear. It's important to both of us, isn't it? It began your life; it certainly changed mine! How proud I was, even if bewildered – I guess not the only one who's felt inadequate to cope with a new life of responsibility – without time off! It's been a long hard road for you, old thing – the learning process still goes on for both of us. I hope we can come to terms with ourselves. A phrase from Dr Albert Schweitzer: "reverence for life". This became a revelation to me, who'd been imprisoned by ideologies and dogma – a liberation into the recognition that all manifestations of life are precious for their own sake – and so was I. Not so much self-esteem but respect for self as part of, interacting with, other lives, other beings, all the processes of Life itself as comprising a whole.'

Dysfunctional Iain's family may have been (and, after all, whose family isn't?), but I am struck by the level of self-awareness they all display. It's this self-awareness which has no doubt enabled them to survive as a family, despite being flung to different parts of the world, and there's no doubt that Iain has been strengthened by it. From self-awareness comes self-belief – and you need a lot of that to keep going as an artist/designer for 25 years.

Next, I contact Welmoed. For 15 years, her life shadowed Iain's, as she lived with him, cooked for him, built boats with him and travelled with him. She seems to have been present at most of the key moments in his later life and probably knows him better than anyone else. We get chatting on the phone, and soon after she sends me wonderful candid photos of him from the past two decades: Iain building the first Acorn 15; Iain and Fabian at the Southampton Boat Show; Iain and Welmoed building *Asphodel*; on their way to meet Peter Spectre; Iain on his motorbike Biggles; Iain packing up to go to Maine; *Jeanie Henderson* being lifted 'oot-the-windae' at Penicuik; Iain moving to Findhorn. The pictures are a fantastic record of Iain's life and present a much more carefree image than Iain's own carefully posed portraits.

She also sends me a graphic description of a crash she and Iain had one snowy night in January 2005. They were driving to Armadale, 50 miles away, to see a movie when the car spun out of control on black ice and Iain, who was driving, was thrown out of the back window, across the road and down a grassy bank. It took passersby and police forty minutes to find him, during which time Welmoed became convinced he had died. He ended up being airlifted by helicopter to Inverness, where he was treated for a crushed vertebra and severe bruises. Later, she sends me detailed descriptions of all the places she visited Iain, where he lived, as she says, 'as a bug under a stone'.

The relationship between Iain and Welmoed is never clearly defined, but as she talks it becomes clear that, at least on her part, it was something more than friendship. She describes him as 'hardworking', 'talented', 'mentally and physically strong' and 'spiritual', and the worst she can say about him is to compare him affectionately to Eeyore. She is 12 years older than Iain, however, and suggests that he was always waiting for his dream (younger) woman to come along and sweep him off his feet. A perfectionist in love, as in everything else, no one was ever good enough.

Eventually, I ask the obvious: was she in love with him? She answers: 'I loved that man very much – absolutely.' Was he a happy man? 'Happy? No! Although he seems more happy recently than I have seen him before.' Was he fanatical? 'Of course! He had to be to do his work.' And we leave it at that.

Peter Spectre is now one of the elder statesmen of the wooden boat movement in the United States, with his hugely successful *Mariners' Book of Days*, and is also editor of the magazine *Maine Boats, Homes and Harbors*. He tells me that he always carries a dictaphone around with him as a kind of oral diary and that he may still have a recording of his second meeting with Iain and Fabian back in 1985. He's been caught out before by a journalist 'borrowing' his material and publishing private details from it though, so he insists on sending the recording to both of them first for approval before releasing it to me.

Six weeks later, I receive a CD in the post with a very scratchy recording of Iain, Fabian and Peter discussing boats, life and the universe. It's amazing to hear them talking together at what was to prove such a pivotal moment for British boatbuilding. There's a great deal of talk about the desirability of British v American working boats, their different approaches to boat design and building, educating people about wood, and Welmoed even makes a cameo appearance, making cups of tea. I'm slightly disappointed to find there's nothing remotely scandalous on the CD, although I am surprised to hear Iain speaking with a startlingly clear English accent. Challenged about this during the interview, he answers that he 'tends to pick up accents' and that he always disliked the Australian accent anyway. At least that explains why he sounds like such a dyed-in-the-wool Scotsman now.

But of the many people I speak to in the subsequent weeks, by far the most eloquent is Iain's one-time colleague Fabian Bush. He talks with great clarity about the development of wooden boatbuilding from a highly professional business with time-served workers to a more amateur-led artisan occupation. He talks of the amateurs 'plugging the holes' left by the professional boatbuilders (who have gone off to make their fortunes building kitchens) and thus keeping the tradition alive.

'It's totally different now,' he says. 'The market for a nice rowing skiff is very small. The people who order new wooden boats now want something very expensive and shiny and covered in brass fittings – the opposite end of our ethos. The only designers who are competitive at the small boat end of the spectrum are people like Swallow Boats, who can work with CAD programs and can produce tailor-made plans and kits very quickly. They're great boats, but not quite what we were thinking of back then.'

Fabian suggests that the greatest threat to that original vision of 'beautiful wooden boats for the masses' may no longer be the competition from fibreglass boats but from the over-simplification of modern technology. Anyone with a CAD (Computer Aided Design) program can now design their dream boat and send their plans to a company with a CNC machine, which can then cut all the components out of sheets of plywood and deliver it back in kit form. It has certainly made wooden boabuilding far more accessible and some of the designs on offer, particularly from Nick and Matthew Newland's Swallow Boats, are as pretty as Iain's – indeed many seem to be simplified versions of his designs. But without Iain's loving attention to detail, there are no guarantees of what the finished boats will turn out like.

For Iain, the threat is very real. At the time of writing, he didn't have a website or even an email address, let alone digital versions of his plans. Approaching his 69th birthday, it seemed a little late in the day for him to be learning about the intricacies of CAD. Yet, with other designers offering customized plans at the push of a button, how much longer will potential boatbuilders be content to buy a set of hand-drawn plans, however beautifully executed? 'It's a niche,' agrees Fabian, 'but Iain's plans still hold their own against anything generated by CAD programs.'

Iain isn't oblivious to the changes. Last year he asked fellow designer Richard Pierce, who lives 130 miles south of Skye on the island of Luing, to run the lines of his Canadian canoe through a CAD program to give him some displacement figures at different angles of heel. He was impressed with how fast the results were generated – even taking into account postage time, it was faster than he could have managed working full time using traditional methods. Later, Richard scanned in the lines of some other canoes and superimposed them over Iain's design in different colours to compare them. Again, Iain was impressed with the improvement over his usual graph method but was doubtful it would be worth the time and expense of getting trained up at his stage of life.

Another parcel arrives with Iain's distinctive handwriting on the front. This one contains more photos, including one of him building his first dory in Bristol in 1980, and a letter.

'Hi Nic, I guess sometimes the feeling of failure is due to, for a long time, lack of resources for building and sailing the boats, not being up to creating a whole series of shallow-draught cruisers, sharpies, trimarans, racing dinghies, and – especially – training dinghies. Being unable to pay a boatbuilder or two to be putting the boats together as I sort out the design. Or, what Nick Newland and Richard Pierce have: the boy growing up and taking over! And maybe some other wee ones to be doing the music, the calligraphy, the aeroplane models, the woodwork, etc etc. Or am I just being greedy? Many things have worked out so well – I've got so much. Just one or two wee things missing still. See ya, Iain.'

More regrets. But the truth is that it is the lack of such things that has made Iain the artist he is. Most creative people – be it artists, writers or designers – start off with ideals which are gradually compromised by the reality of keeping a roof over one's head, feeding oneself, keeping the customer satisfied and maintaining relationships, family and social networks. Few have such belief in their work that they are willing to sacrifice one or all of these things, as Iain plainly has done. After all, how many women would put up with a partner who works 10–12 hours a day at his drawing board and seems to barely feel the need for such basic human requirements as food, drink and an occasional holiday?

Yet, even as far back as 1986, in Peter Spectre's article for *WoodenBoat* magazine, Iain worried about betraying his principles, saying: 'In many ways I have compromised too much, and this makes compromises harder to accept.' Such is the purity of his vision.

The ever-eloquent Fabian Bush, who himself compromised his ideals to some extent and took on boat repair and restoration work in order to survive as a boatbuilder, expresses this conundrum well, and it is worth repeating what he said as it sums up the path that, deliberately or not, Iain has chosen: 'I always regarded Iain as an artist. He was being an individualist and an enthusiast, and he wasn't interested in material wealth. He lived on no money, but he had to do that in order to focus on his work. Because, as soon as you start thinking about ways of earning money, then you get diverted from the main task. It's only by living like that, that he could achieve what he achieved.'

appendix I
COMPLETE LIST OF OUGHTRED DESIGNS

No	Name	Length	Type	Year	Notes
1	*Happy Jack*	18ft	Centreboard sloop	1967	Commissioned by CE Boden, built
2	*La Sirene*	30ft	Trimaran	1968	
3	*Duifken I*	29ft	Double-ended cutter	1974	Commissioned by Jan de Voogd
4	No name	N/A	Canoe yawl	1976	
5	*Mermaid*	30ft	Trimaran	1976	Model built
6	*Duyfken*	29ft 5in	Double-ended cutter	1977	Commissioned by Jan de Voogd, built
7	*Earwig*	11ft	Moth dinghy	1977	Built
8	*Magic Fish*	11ft	Moth dinghy	1978	
9	*Gipsy Queen*	41ft 8in	Clipper-bowed ketch	1978	Half-model built
10	No name	38ft	Cutter	1979	
11	No name	24ft	Sloop	1979	Half-model built
12	No name	27ft 6in	Cat yawl	1980	
13	No name	15ft 4in	Light dory	1980	Built
14	*Seahorse*	15ft	Flat-bottomed skiff	1980	Built
15	*Flying Fish*	18ft	Flat-bottomed skiff	1981	
16	*Oyster*	13ft	Sailing dinghy	1981	
17	*Mackerel*	15ft 4in	Dory	1981	Built
18	*Barnacle*	10ft	Pram dinghy	1981	
19	*Blackfish Dory*	15ft 4in	Dory	1981	Built
20	*Pike*	12ft	Flat-bottomed skiff	1982	Built
21	*Acorn Skiff*	11ft 9in	Centreplate skiff	1982	Built
22	*Acorn 15*	15ft	Centreplate skiff	1982	Built
23	*Acorn Pram*	7ft 9in	Pram dinghy	1982	Built
24	No name	8ft 6in	Pram dinghy	1982	Commission, built
25	*John Dory*	18ft 1in	Swampscott dory	1983	Built
26	No name	25ft	Racing dory	1983	
27	No name	32ft 7in	Cat yawl	1983	
28	No name	21ft	Steam dory	1983	Commissioned by Ewan Strathcona, built
29	No name	40ft	Junk-rigged schooner	1983	Commission
30	*Acorn 16*	16ft	Sailing dinghy	1983	Commission, built
31	*Acorn Dinghy*	10ft 2in	Dinghy	1984	Built
32	*Auk*	7ft 10in	Dinghy	1984	Ex-Wren, also Acorn Tender, built

No	Name	Length	Type	Year	Notes
33	*MacGregor*	13ft 7in	Sail/paddle canoe	1986	Built
34	*Wee Rob*	12ft	Sail/paddle canoe	1986	Built
35	No name	17ft	Sailing canoe	1986	
36	No name	27ft	River launch	1986	Commissioned by Charles Fairbrother
37	*Zeina II*	30ft	River launch	1986	Commission, built
38	*Grey Seal*	22ft	Gunter-rigged sloop	1986–8	Built
39	*Erika*	19ft	Beach boat	1988	Commissioned by Peter Mumford, built
40	*Grey Seal*	22ft	Bermudan sloop	1988	Built
41	*Amberjack*	15ft 9in	Dory	1988	Ex-Stickleback, built
42	*Scorcher*	24ft	Steel steam house boat	1988	Commissioned by Charles Fairbrother
43	*Fulmar*	16ft 8in	Sailing dinghy	1988–9	Ex-Silver Gull, built
44	*Granny Pram*	9ft 4in	Pram dinghy	1988	Built
45	*Mouse Pram*	7ft 9in	Pram dinghy	1988	Built
46	*Caledonia Yawl*	19ft 3in	Beach boat	1988	Built
47	*Shearwater*	11ft 10in	Sailing dinghy	1989	Ex-Egret, built
48	*Ness Boat*	16ft 6in	Beach boat	1989	Built
49	*Gannet*	14ft 6in	Sailing dinghy	1990	Built
50	*Whilly Boat*	14ft 6in	Beach boat	1990	Built
51	*Feather*	6ft 8in	Pram dinghy	1990	Built
52	*Mole*	16ft	Rowing skiff	1990	Built
53	No name	10ft 4in	Canoe	1991	
54	*Guillemot*	11ft 6in	Clinker dinghy	1991	Ex-Ptarmigan, built
55	*Pragmatist*	24ft	Steel punt	1991	Commissioned by Charles Fairbrother, built
56	*Tammie Norrie*	13ft 6in	Clinker dinghy	1991	Ex-Grebe, built
57	No name	11ft	Dory skiff	1992	
58	*Badger*	19ft	River skiff	1992	Built
59	*Ness Yawl*	19ft 2in	Beach boat	1992	Built
60	*Wee Seal*	18ft	Double-ended sloop	1992	Built
61	No name	26ft	Electric launch	1992	Built
62	No name	16ft	Sneakbox	1992	Built
63	*Humble Bee*	7ft 9in	Pram dinghy	1993	Built
64	*Farne Islander*	20ft	Gaff cutter	1995	Commissioned by McNulty Boats, built
65	No name	13ft 6in	Cat-rigged dinghy	1995	Commissioned by Rudi Greiser
66	*Henry St Clair*	60ft	Birlinn	1995	Model built
67	*Snipefish*	15ft 6in	Outrigger skiff	1996	Commissioned by John Lowe, built
68	*I Mo Cridhe*	20ft	Motor sailer	1996	Commissoned by Harold Troup, built
69	*Eun na Mara*	19ft 9in	Canoe yawl	1997	Commissioned by Brice Avery, also *Minna*, built
70	*Puffin*	10ft 2in	Dinghy	1997	Ex-Robin, built

No	Name	Length	Type	Year	Notes
71	*Beaver*	16ft	Canadian canoe	1997	Built
72	*Elf*	15ft	Faering	1998	Built
73	*Wee Ness Yawl*	18ft 2in	Beach boat	1998	95% version of Ness Yawl
74	No name	19ft 6in	Sark-Jersey racer	1998	Built
75	*Mr Jones*	19ft 6in	Beach boat	1999	7-strake version of Cal Yawl for Cedric Jones, built
76	No name	48ft	Birlinn	1999	Model built
77	No name	17ft	Yawl	1999	Commissioned by CH Caitlin, built
78	*Scoraig Skiff*	22ft	West Coast skiff	1999	Commissioned by Topher Dawson
79	No name	11ft 6in	Flat-bottomed dinghy	2000	
80	*JII*	18ft 2in	Beach boat	2000	Built
81	*Wee Rob II*	12ft	Canoe	2001	Built
82	*Wee Seal II*	18ft 6in	Sloop	2002	Built
83	*Lochgilphead Skiff*	17ft 4in	Skiff	2002	Built
84	No name	17ft 1in	Yawl	2002	Built
85	No name	13ft	Dory skiff	2002	
86	*Arctic Tern*	18ft 2in	Beach boat	2002	Built
87	*Haiku*	30ft	Sharpie	2002	Commissioned by Alastair Bremner, built
88	*Galewei Faering*	16ft 6in	Traditional faering	2002	Commissioned by Colin Galloway, built
89	*Elfyn*	16ft 6in	Plywood faering	2003	Built
90	*Pt Bannatyne Skiff*	15ft	Skiff	2003	Commissioned by Maldwin Drummond, built
91	*Tirrik*	17ft	Beach boat	2003	Built
92	*Whilly Tern*	15ft	Beach boat	2004	Built
93	*Skerrieskiff*	15ft	Beach boat	2004	Built
94	*Skerrieskiff 17*	17ft	Beach boat	2004	Built
95	*JII MkII*	18ft 2in	Beach boat	2004	Built
96	*Caledonia Yawl II*	19ft 6in	Beach boat	2004	Built
97	*Caledonia Yawl III*	19ft 6in	Beach boat	2005	Built
98	*Wee Rob Mk III*	12ft 2in	Canoe	2005	Built
99	*Stickleback*	10ft 8in	Canoe	2005	Built
100	*Woodfish*	15ft 3in	Faering	2005	Built
101	*MacGregor MkII*	14ft	Canoe	2006	Built
102	*Spike*	12ft 2in	Skiff	2006	
103	*Sula*	18ft	Shetland Yoal	2007	Commissioned by John Levell, built
104	*Super Seal*	24ft 7in	Cruising yacht	2007	
105	*Auklet*	7ft	Dinghy	2008	Built
106	*Penny Fee*	16ft	Dinghy	2008	
107	*John Pear*	18ft 4in	Norwegian faering	2009	Commissioned by John Pear, built

appendix II
THE PLANS (A SELECTION)

PRAMS

Pram dinghies often get a poor press, probably because of their diminutive size and the feeling that their design is too much of a compromise to be really efficient. Yet it's a type that has fascinated Iain since he first started designing boats in earnest. His first pram dates back to the Barnacle design of 1981, and he has created at least six more since then. The inspiration for his successful Mouse Pram came from seeing countless Nutshells being built at the *WoodenBoat*

boatbuilding school during his sabbatical there in 1986.

He explains his fascination with the type in his design notes for the Granny Pram: 'The pram dinghy is one of the most difficult boats to design, because of the limitations of the overall size. Any boat design is a compromise; the pram is several compromises. She must be light but take rough treatment; perform well single-handed but carry several people safely, tracking well when rowing or towing. In this case, the boat had to be simple and quick to

build for inexperienced amateurs.'

Although Iain's initial priority was to simplify the concept for amateur construction, doing away with any internal frames and all laminated parts, he later developed the design for traditional construction. The 6ft 8in Feather Pram has a round-bilged hull with eight strakes per side (compared to just four on the Mouse and Granny prams). Just like the 7ft 9in Humble Bee, which followed in 1993, it can just as well be built out of cedar or spruce as out of plywood.

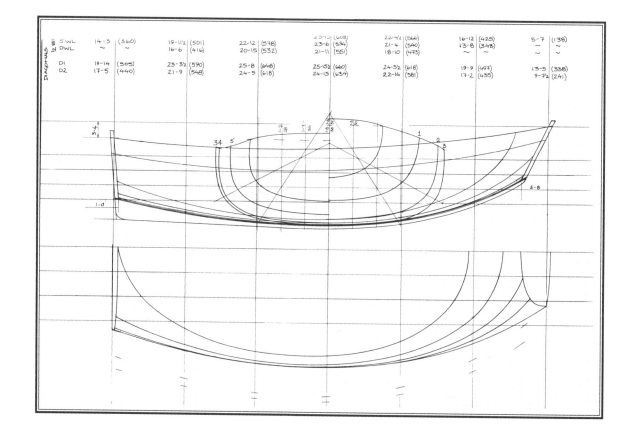

◻ Humble Bee ◻ Granny

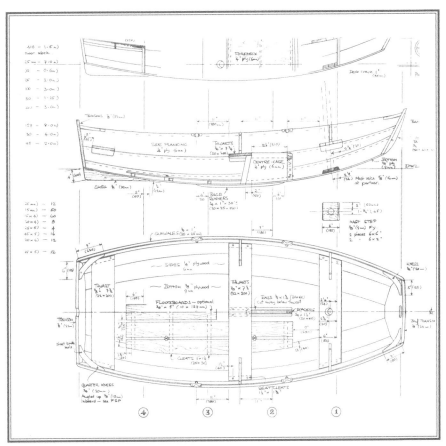

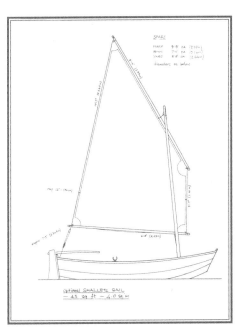

OPTIONAL SMALLER SAIL
— 43 sq ft ~ 4.0 sq m

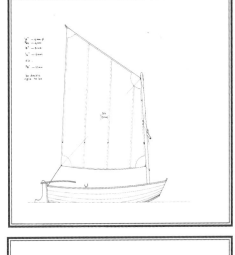

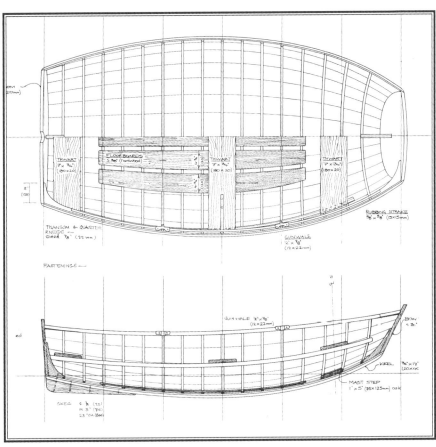

humble be
sail plan

CANOES, ROWING AND RIVER BOATS

It was the adventures of the Scottish philanthropist (and, according to some, religious zealot) John MacGregor and his Rob Roy designs that popularized sailing canoes in the late 1800s, particularly in North America. The boats have also been an object of enduring fascination for Iain, who suggests that 'the fun per pound (weight) or pound (money), or hours of preparation, may be far ahead of any other type of boat.'

In particular, he was intrigued by the huge amount of research that went into developing different rigs for sailing canoes. And indeed the boats do present the designer with a unique challenge: their intrinsic lack of stability means that the centre of effort of the rig has to be very low and/or spread between two masts. The limited space on board means the crew can't move

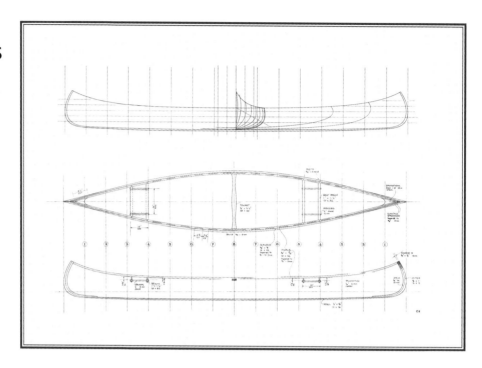

around as freely as in other types of boat, which has led to all kinds of clever contraptions for hoisting, stowing and reefing sails while under way.

The MacGregor Canoe (and its smaller sister the Wee Rob) was Iain's first attempt at designing a

sailing canoe and comes with the option of a battened balanced lug rig or a more unusual-looking fully-battened gunter rig. As well as redrawing all his old canoe plans (including a written sheet of instructions for adapting them for traditional construction), Iain

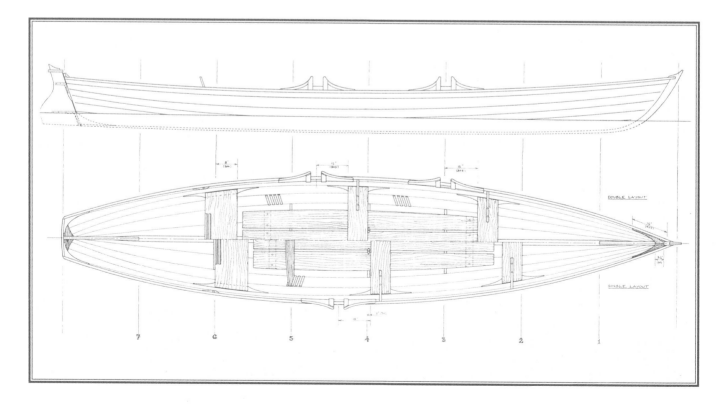

☐ Beaver   ☐ Badger

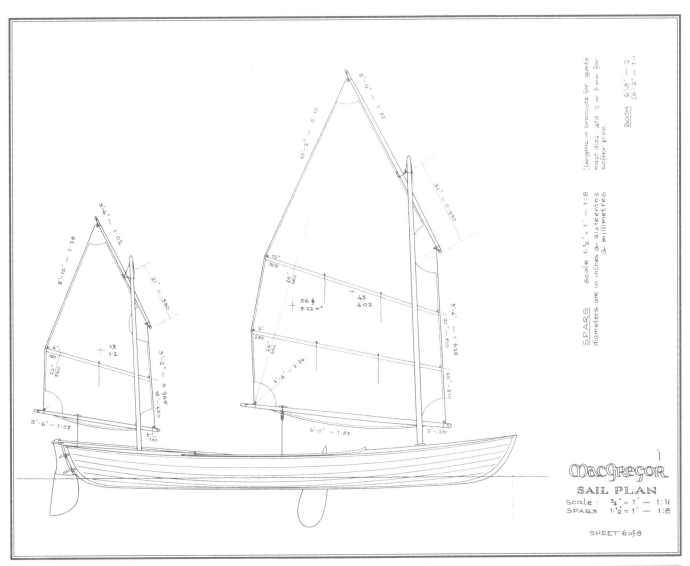

MacGregor

SAIL PLAN

Scale: ¾" = 1' ~ 1:16
SPARS 1½" = 1' ~ 1:8

SHEET 6 of 8

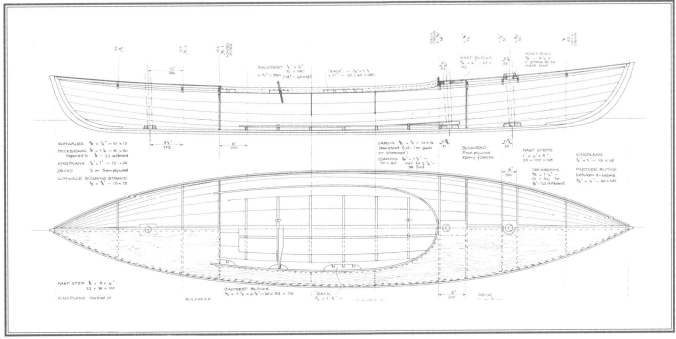

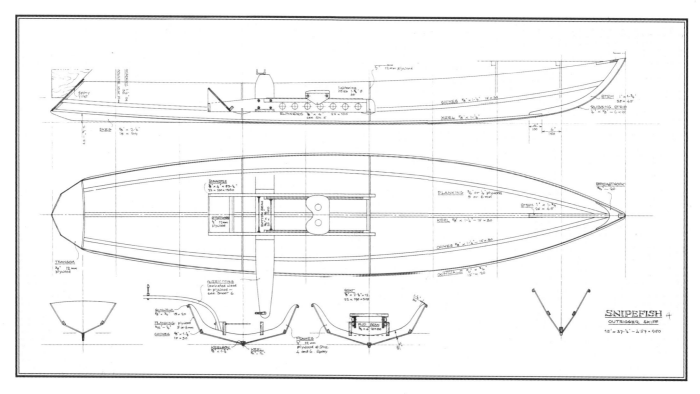

recently came up with a new design: the 10ft 8in Stickleback (not to be confused with the 15ft 9in dory of the same name, now renamed the Amberjack) which he planned to build for himself.

By contrast, Iain has only had one shot at designing a Canadian canoe: the 16ft Beaver. In his design notes, he describes the many hours that went into drawing the lines, rubbing them out and refining them, again and again. Drawing the mid section, he had to strike a balance between speed and stability, while the rocker was a compromise between manoeuvrability and tracking. The result, he says, is a Canadian canoe 'of approximately perfect form and proportion'. We agree!

The other two boats in this group represent two extremes: a traditional Thames skiff and a modern rowing machine. With the 19ft Badger, Iain again tried to strike a balance, this time between the hardcore sculls used for racing on

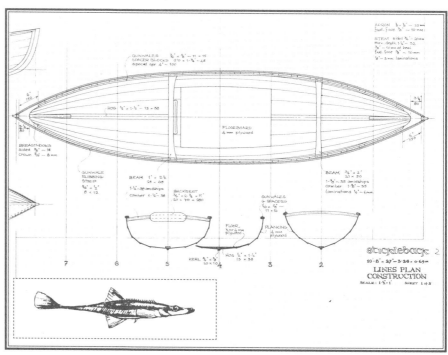

rivers and the ubiquitous 'family' picnic boats. The result is a lightweight rowing craft which fairly skims across the water and yet has enough stability to be used for messing about on the river. The 15ft Snipefish, on the other hand, is all

about rowing – although, being designed to survive the surf that builds up at the entrance of Findhorn Harbour, it does have more seagoing capability than most of its ilk.

☐ Snipefish   ☐ Stickleback

TRADITIONAL DINGHIES

This was where it all started for Iain, in terms of his burgeoning boat design career. The Acorn Skiff was the first round-bilged clinker boat he designed and the first he built using epoxy. The design caught the eye of Maynard Bray at *WoodenBoat*, who wrote it up in the magazine – and the rest is history. Iain based the design on the famous American Whitehall boats but admits that the waterline turned out a bit narrower than he had intended, meaning that the Acorn Skiff turned into more of a performance boat than its original muse.

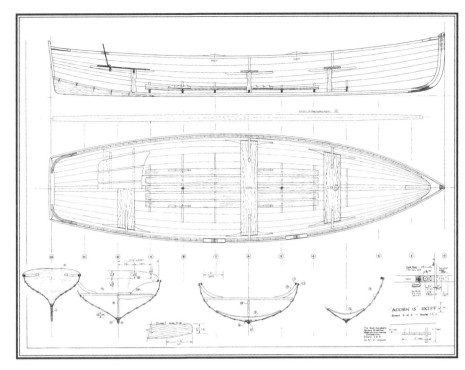

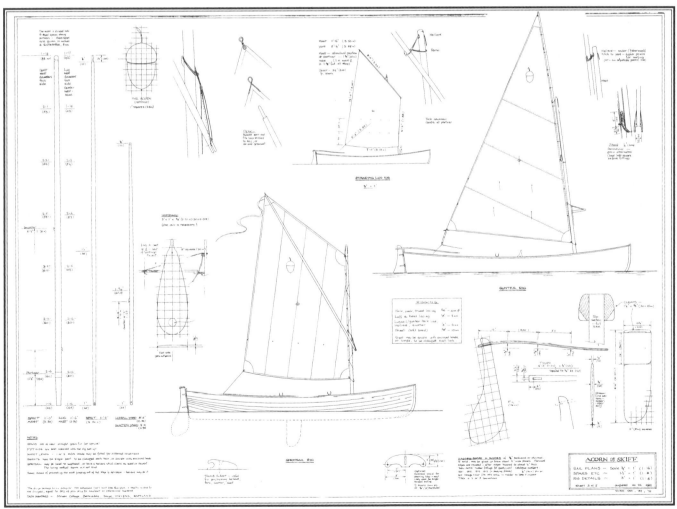

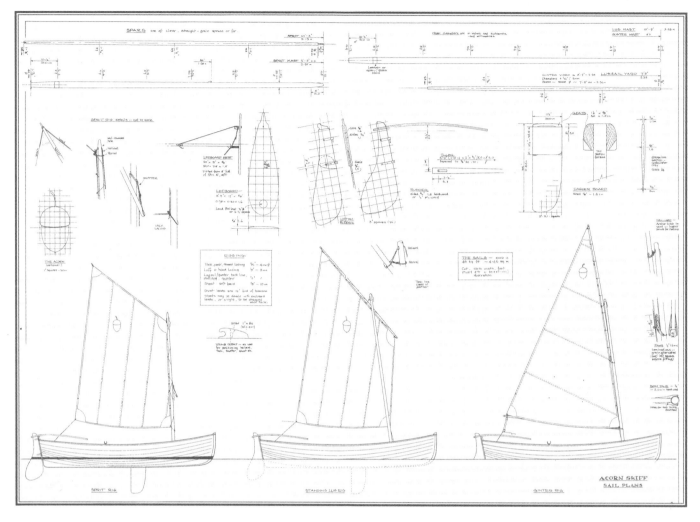

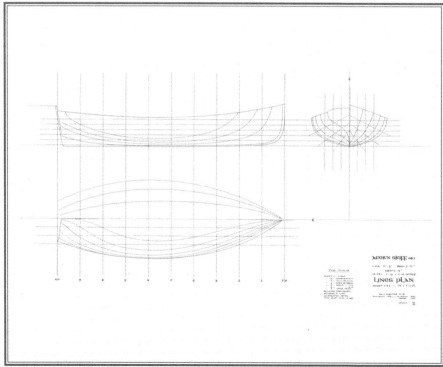

The Acorn 13 is a stretched version of the original 12-footer, while the Acorn 15 is a separate design – although obviously closely related. Both boats are offered with the option of either a sprit, gunter or lug rig and, fitted with a dagger board or leeboard, give a good (if slightly nervy) performance under sail. Iain points out that the boats are more responsive and manoeuvrable than traditional designs of the type, due not only to their lighter weight but also to the added rocker on the keel.

Despite the success of the Acorn Skiff and its progeny, Iain knew there was a demand for a similar boat with a slightly more

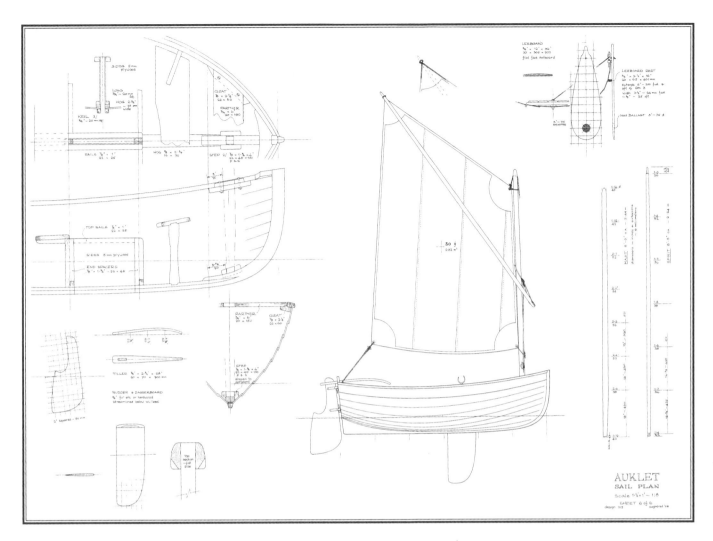

AUKLET
SAIL PLAN
Scale 1½"=1'=1:8
SHEET 6 of 6
design 103   oughtred '96

'burdensome' hull. The answer was the 11ft 6in Guillemot (originally called the Ptarmigan) which he designed in 1991. With flatter floors, firmer bilges and a higher freeboard, the design isn't quite as nippy as its predecessors, but it is steadier and can carry a load. The Guillemot spawned the 2ft longer Tammie Norrie, and the two are now the bestselling boats in the Oughtred catalogue. As this book went to press, he was finalizing the design for a 16ft version, to be called the Penny Fee.

The smallest in the range is the 8ft Auk, designed primarily as a yacht tender, and a chunkier, sweeter little boat it would be hard

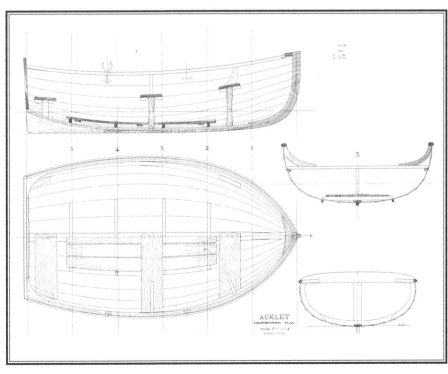

AUKLET
CONSTRUCTION PLAN
Scale 3"=1'=1:4

to imagine. Iain's favourite story about this design involves a group of three adults and four children, who all piled into their Auk and went cruising for several days on a river in Australia – and he has the pictures to prove it! *Classic Boat* columnist Niki Perryman stretched the design to 9ft as a tender for her boat. Iain is following suit with a long version at the same time as going in the other direction with the 7ft Auklet.

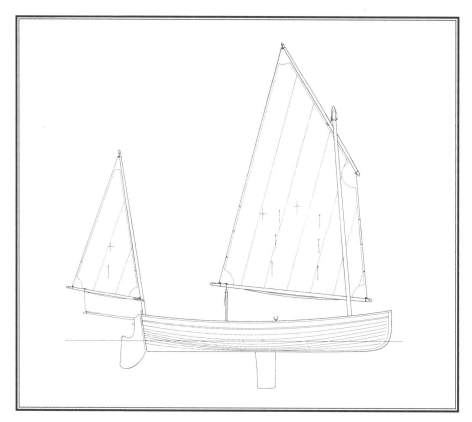

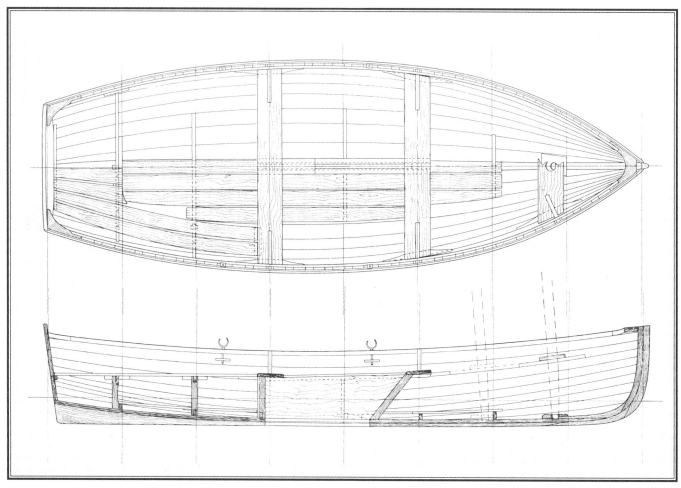

SAILING DINGHIES

Iain's idea with the 16ft 8in Fulmar
was to provide a traditional
alternative to the Wayfarer dinghy –
only better. His boat would be more
able, more seaworthy, more
comfortable, drier and safer.
Certainly the flat run aft, with a
broad transom, firm bilges and
larger sailing rig announce that this
is, in Iain's words, a 'proper sailing
boat'. Rowing is only recommended
for moderate distances, although
the hull shape does lend itself to
taking an outboard. Given the right
conditions, this boat will plane!

At over 16ft, the Fulmar is a lot

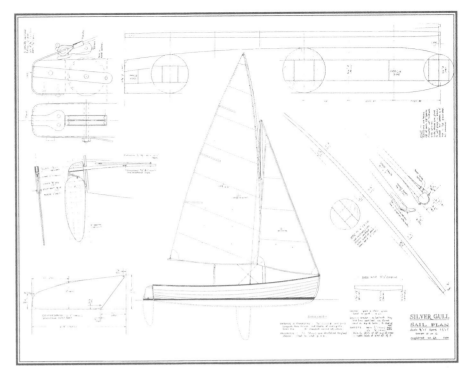

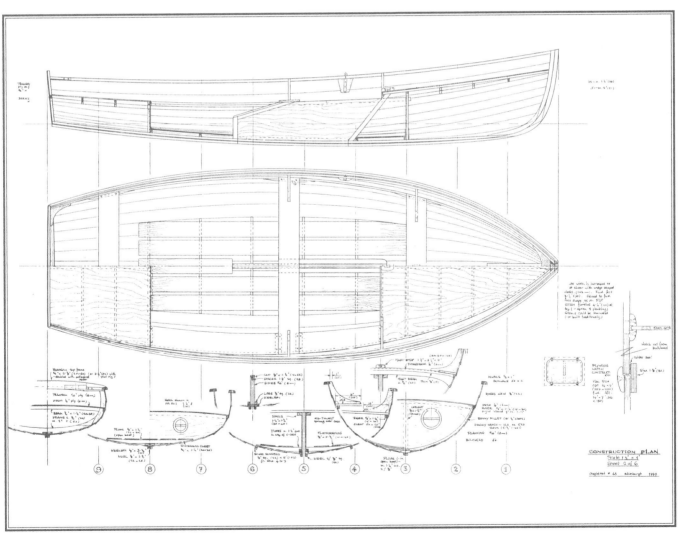

of boat, however, and Iain subsequently drew two smaller versions: the 14ft 5in Gannet and the 11ft 10in Shearwater. All three are at the more modern end of Iain's design spectrum and are no doubt partly inspired by his days racing dinghies on Sydney Harbour. In each case, the builder is faced with a choice. He or she can either go for the more traditional option of an open hull with a lug or gaff rig, or choose the modern alternative of a half-decked hull and gunter or bermudan rig – or any combination of the two. Certainly, the half-decked version (complete with built-in buoyancy) looks like the more hard-working and would make a great little cruising boat.

As ever, Iain has gone to great pains to simplify the design for amateur construction and reckons the Shearwater should only take 200 hours or so to build, compared to 360 hours for the Fulmar – not including the rig. Some floors are fitted, in order to keep the bottom planking light, and he suggests making the stem from sawn sections, to avoid having to laminate any parts.

(NB Iain's time estimates are for professional builders; amateur builders may take up to twice as long.)

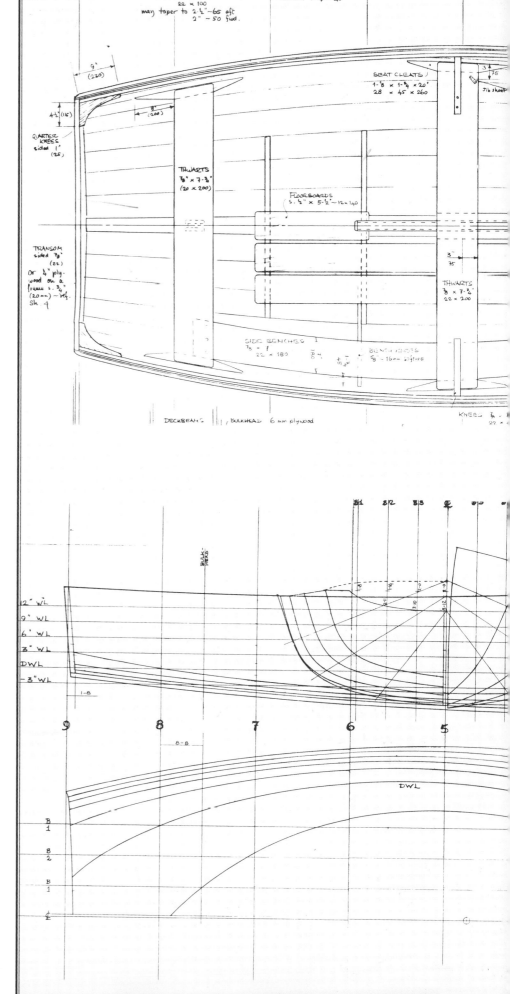

☐ Gannet

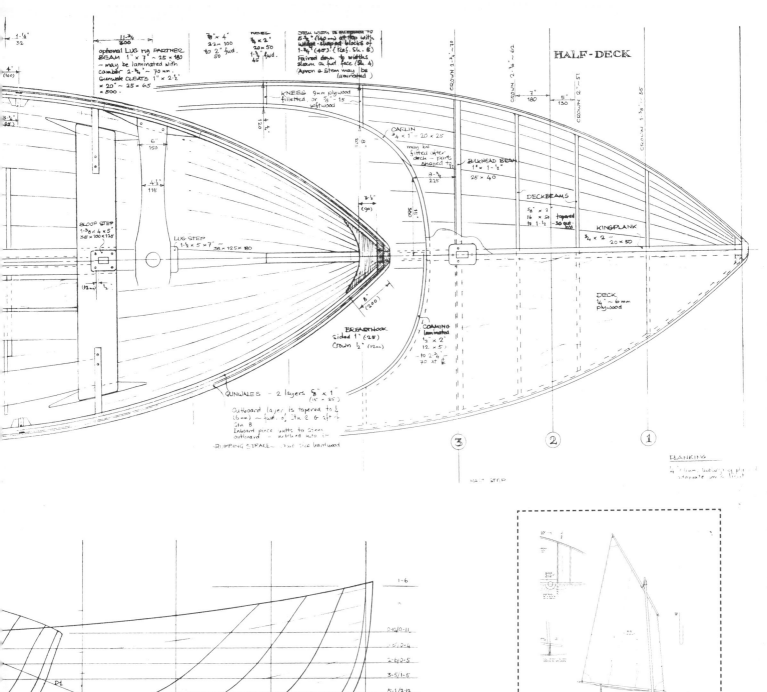

HALF-DECK

optional LUG rig PARTNER
BEAM 1" × 7" ~ 25 × 180
— may be laminated with
camber 2¾" ~ 70 mm.
Gunwale CLEATS 1" × 2½"
× 20" ~ 25 × 65
× 500.

KNEES 9mm plywood
filletted, or ⅝" ~ 15
softwood

CARLIN
¾ × 1 ~ 20 × 25
may be
fitted after
deck — parts
shaped to

BULKHEAD BEAM
1" × 1-½"
25 × 40

CROWN 2-¾ ~ 70

CROWN 2-½ ~ 62

CROWN 2" ~ 51

7"
180

5"
130

CROWN 1⅜ ~ 55

DECKBEAMS
⅝" × 2"
16 × 50 tapered
to 1 ½ ~ 30 out

KINGPLANK
¾ × 2 ~
20 × 50

SLOOP STEP
1-⅜ × 4 × 5"
38 × 100 × 125

LUG STEP
1-½ × 5 × 7" ~
38 × 125 × 180

DECK
¼" ~ 6mm
plywood

BREASTHOOK
Sided 1" (25)
Crown ½" (12mm)

COAMING
laminated
½" × 2"
12 × 50
— to 2-¾"
70 at ℄

GUNWALES — 2 layers ⅝" × 1"
(15 ~ 25)

Outboard layer is tapered to ¼
(6mm) ~ fwd. o' Stn 2 & aft +
Stn 8
Inboard piece butts to Stem
outboard ~ scribed into

RUBBING STRAKE

MAST STEP

PLANKING

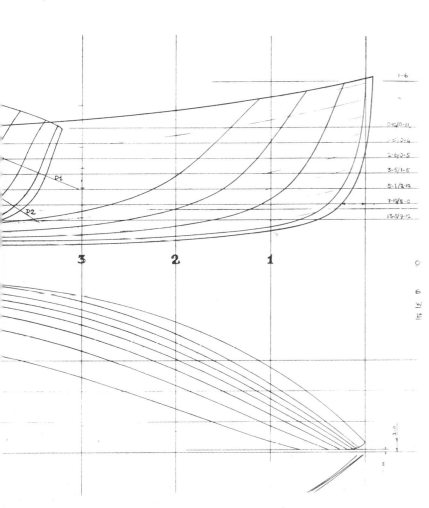

1-6

0-14/0-11

3-5/1-5

5-1/2-12

7-12/5-0

13-5/9-12

3   2   1

D1

D2

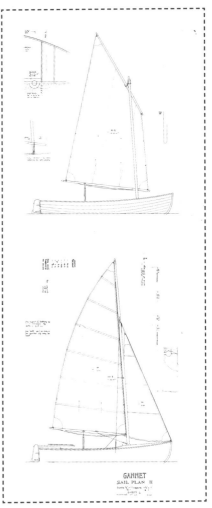

GANNET
SAIL PLAN II

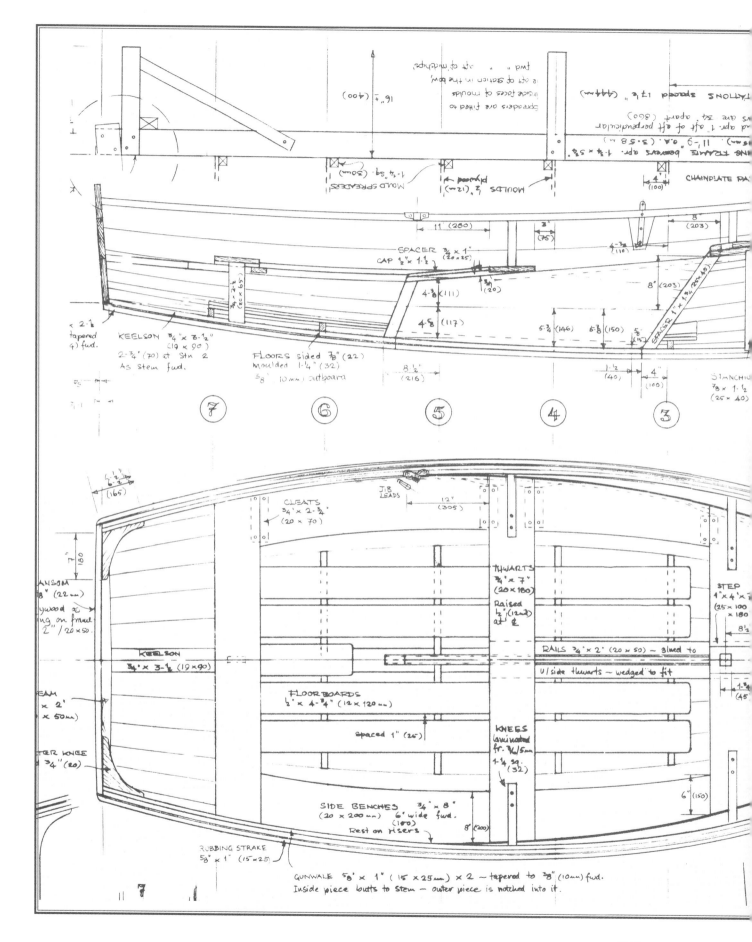

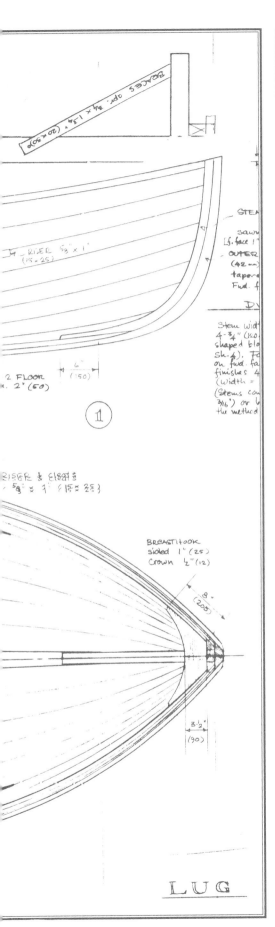

BRACES apr. ¾ × 1¾ (20 × 50)

J RISER ⅝ × 1"
(15 × 25)

2 FLOOR
k. 2" (50)

|← 6" →|
(150)

①

RISER & CLEATS
⅝" × 1" (15 × 25)

BREASTHOOK
sided 1" (25)
Crown ½" (12)

8"
(205)

3½"
(90)

LUG

STE...

sawr...
l.f. face 1"...
OUTER...
(42 mm)
taper...
Fwd. f...

D...

Stem widt...
4-¾" (120...
shaped blo...
Sh. 4). Fo...
on fwd. fa...
finishes 4...
(Width =...
(Stems co...
3/16") or...
the method...

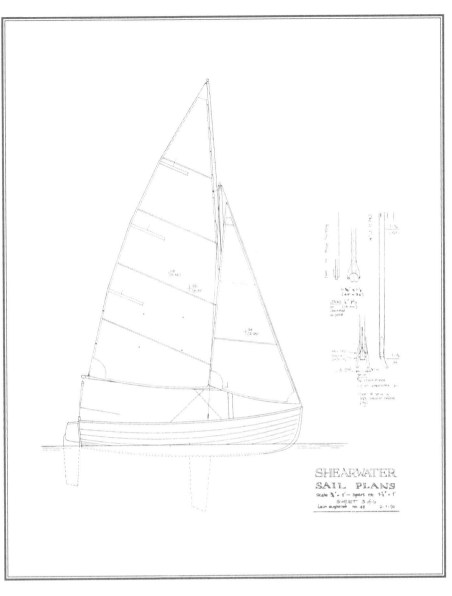

SHEARWATER
SAIL PLANS
Scale ¾" - 1' – spars etc 1½" = 1'
SHEET 3 of 5
Iain oughtred   no. 47   2-1-90

DORIES

When it comes to amateur boatbuilding, you can't get much simpler than a dory. Quick and cheap to build, dories are nevertheless surprisingly seaworthy – as witnessed by the hundreds of them built to fish the Grand Banks in the second half of the 19th century. Yet Iain reckons his 15ft Mackerel takes just 120 hours to build and only costs around £500 in materials, excluding the rig.

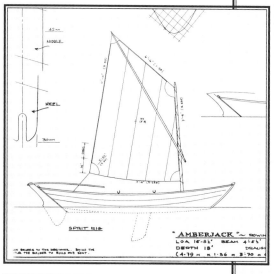

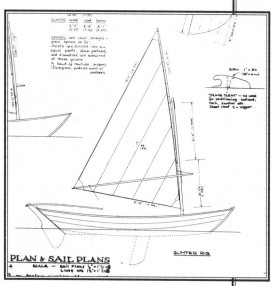

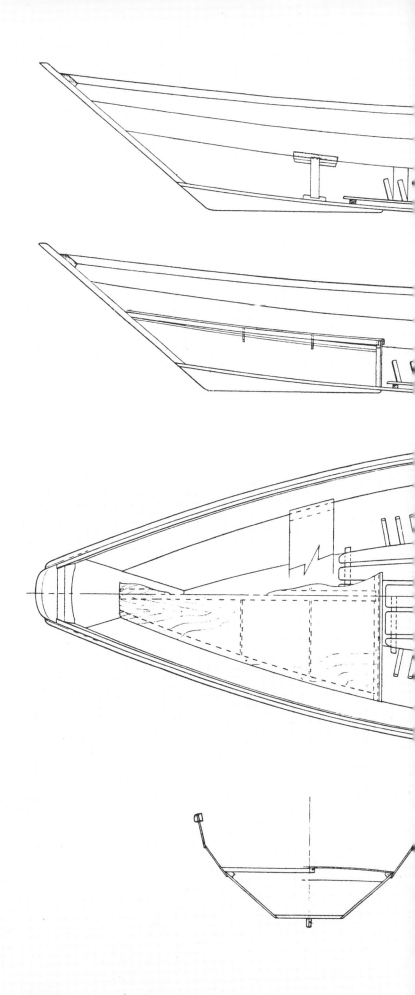

 Amberjack

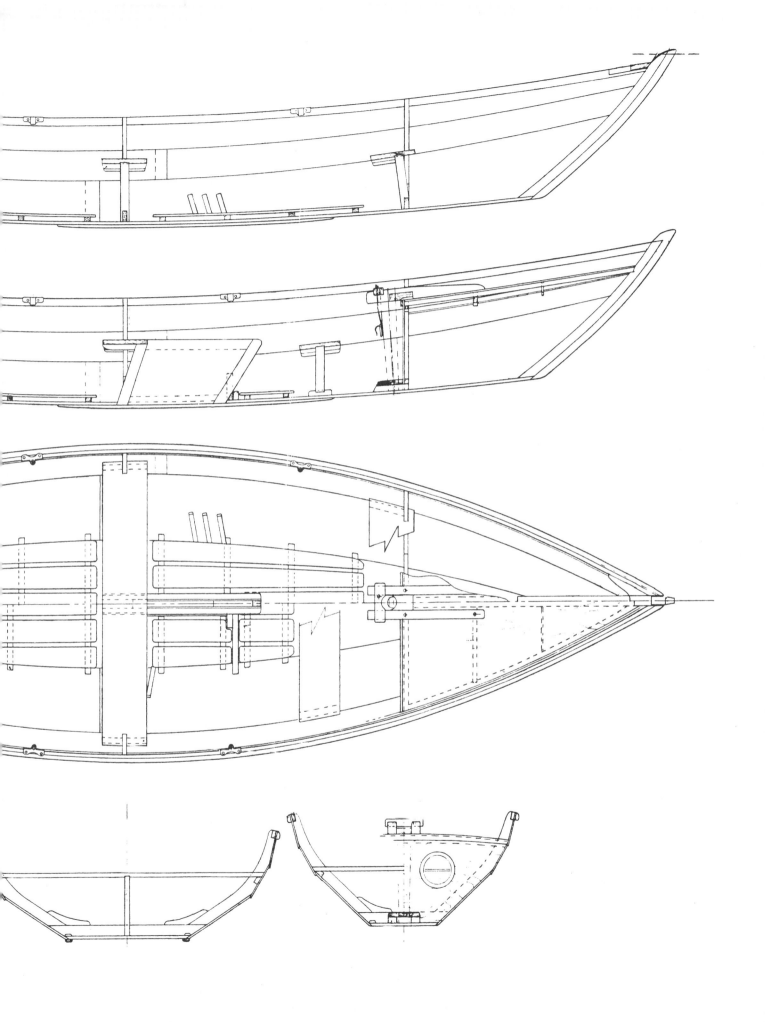

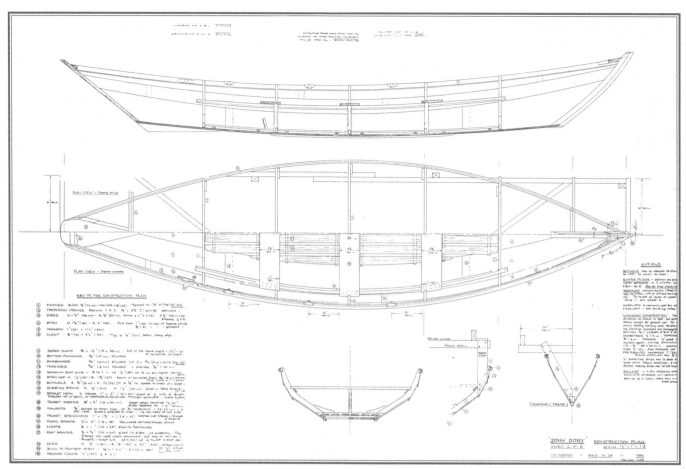

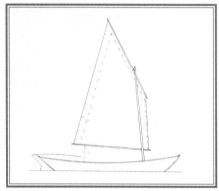
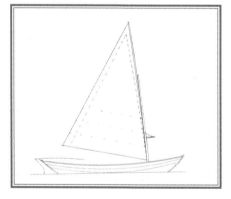
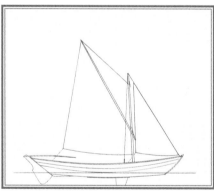

It's not surprising then that when he launched his career as a boat designer, he chose a dory as one of his first designs. Inspired by his meeting with Phil Bolger in Maine in 1981, Iain designed and built his Blackfish dory in Bristol and advertised the plans for sale in *Practical Boat Owner* magazine. With its narrow waterline beam and lack of stability, the Blackfish is a better rowing boat than a sailboat –

although it does come with the option of a sprit, lug or gunter rig. Nearly 30 years later, the plans still feature in his catalogue.

Slightly more sophisticated is the John Dory, which Iain built for Alastair Bremner in 1983. Based on the Swampscott dory design, this 18ft 3in dinghy has rounded topsides, which make it a little more complicated to build than the Banks-style dory but improves its

stability and makes for better performance both under oar and sail. Iain sailed the prototype *Asphodel* in the Scilly Isles with the new owner, and the resulting photos featured in several magazines, helping to launch his career. He later designed the slightly smaller 15ft 8in Amberjack (formerly the Stickleback), as an enhanced alternative to the original Blackfish.

DOUBLE-ENDERS

Little did Iain know, when he started drawing the Caledonia Yawl in London in the winter of 1987 (and later that year in Ireland), that he was embarking on a major new strand of designs. His double-ended 'beach boats', including all their variants, now number more than a dozen, and many people now know him primarily as the designer of 'Shetland boats'. Part of this success can be attributed to the emergence of the so-called 'raids' (coastal cruises/races in open boats) to which Iain's double-enders have proven particularly well suited. Indeed, it

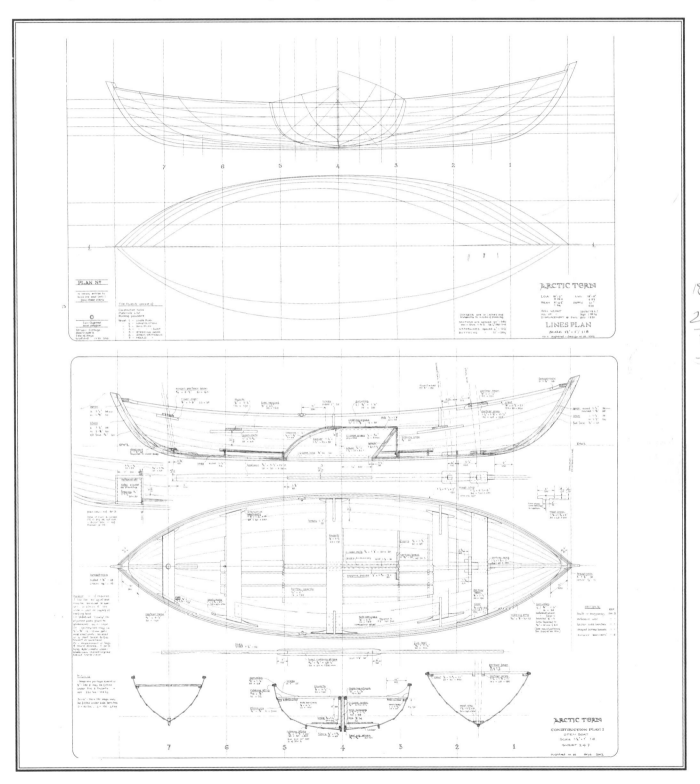

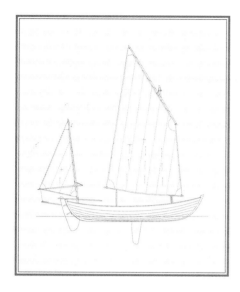

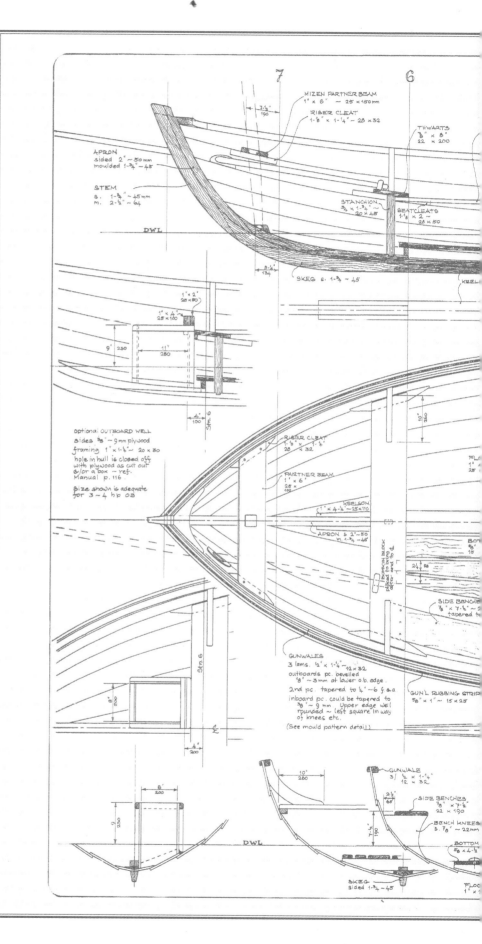

would be hard to imagine a raid without at least a smattering of Oughtred designs – sometimes with Iain on board and usually at the top of the leaderboards!

This means the boats have been tried and tested to a high degree, which has allowed Iain to refine his drawings in the light of lessons learned on the water. There has also been a growing demand for plans of traditional versions of the boats – ie round-bilge versions to be built out of either plywood or solid timber – which Iain seems to have developed a preference for. The result is that all the boats have been through several mutations and the range now available differs quite considerably from the designs Iain drew 20 years ago.

The original boats that Iain drew in the late 1980s were the 19ft 6in Caledonia Yawl, the 16ft 6in Ness Boat and the 14ft 6in Whilly Boat. These were rugged, seaworthy dayboats, with four strakes per side, designed as much for rowing as sailing. A few years later, he drew a leaner, meaner version of the Ness Boat for himself, which became the popular 19ft 2in Ness Yawl.

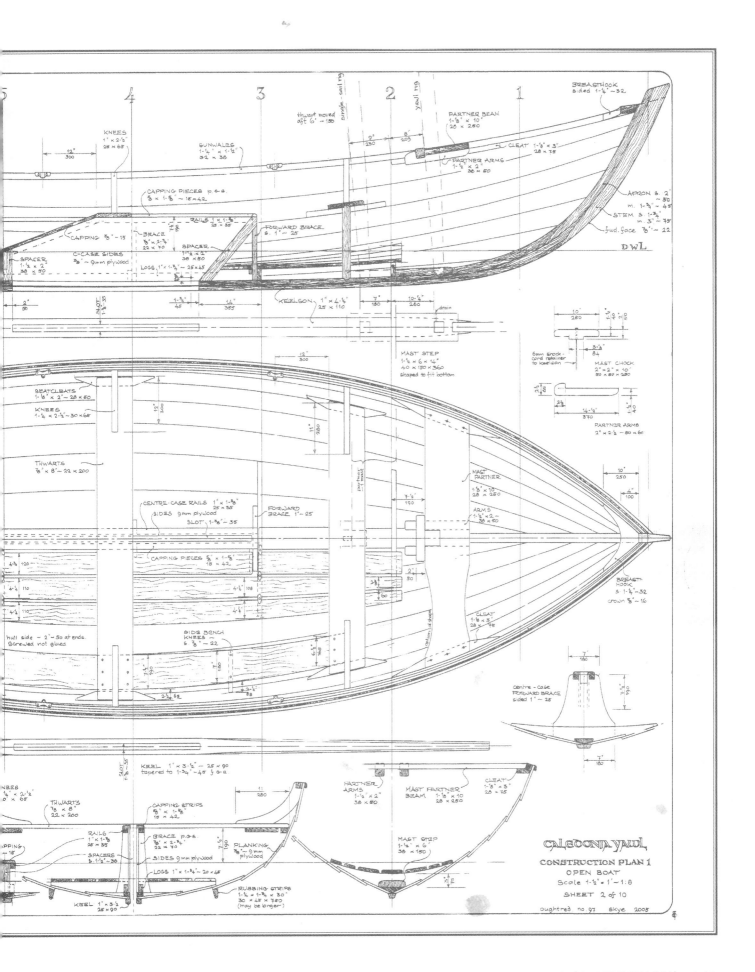

CALEDONIA YAWL

CONSTRUCTION PLAN 1
OPEN BOAT
Scale 1-½" = 1' – 1:8
SHEET 2 of 10

oughtred no.97   skye 2005

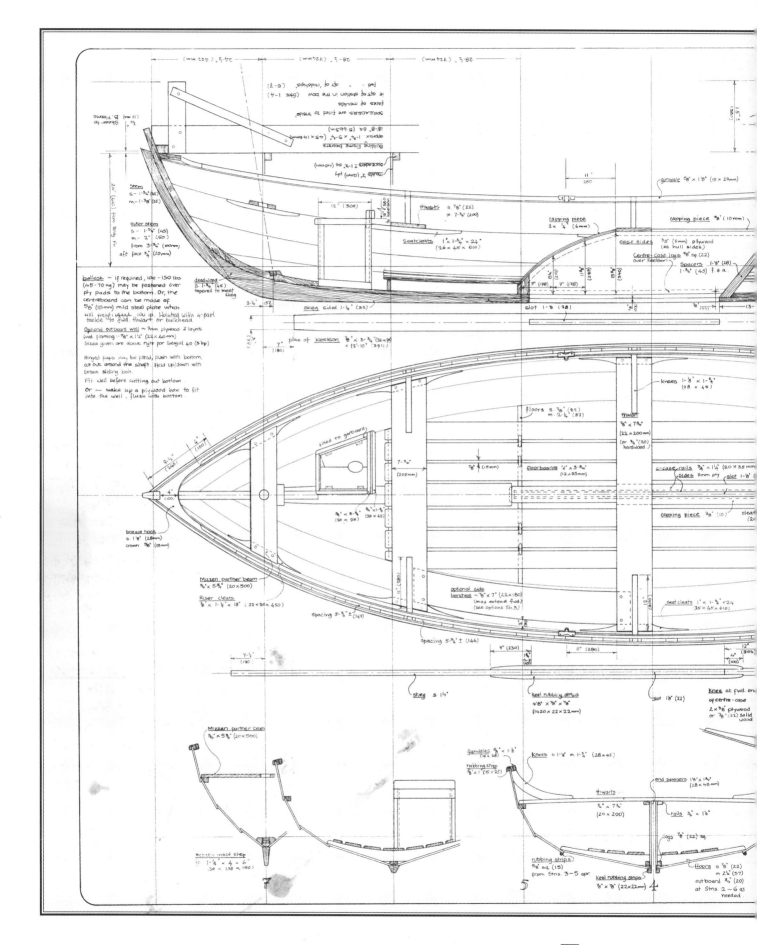

Ness Yawl

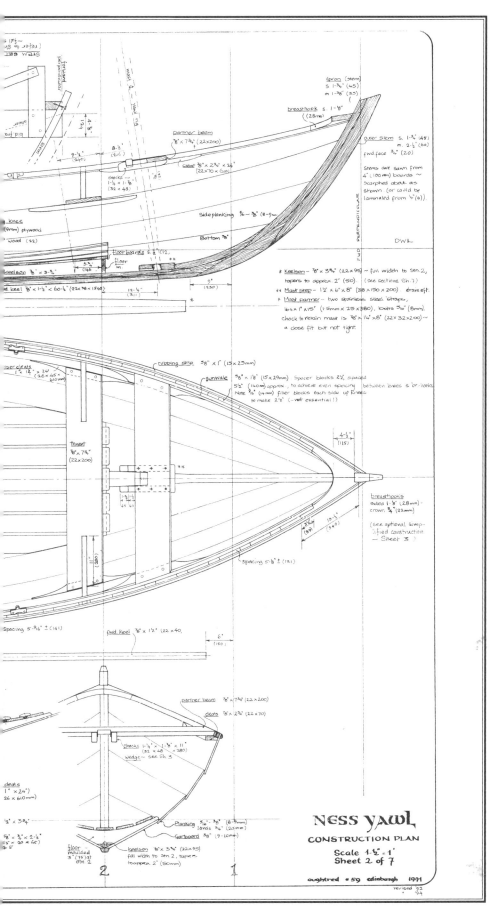

NESS YAWL
CONSTRUCTION PLAN
Scale 1-½" = 1'
Sheet 2 of 7

oughtred • 59 edinburgh 1991
revised '92
'94

The first seven-strake version came in 1999, which was a Caledonia Yawl for a customer in Germany. That was followed by a scaled-down version of the Ness Yawl called the Jeanie II, which Iain again built for himself and on which he subsequently won the 2003 Glen Raid. Redrawn with a round bilge and six strakes per side, the *Jeanie II* later became the Arctic Tern.

By then, Iain had realized that his original vision (where these boats were being rowed as much as they were sailed) wasn't happening in practice. Instead, the narrow waterlines he had drawn with rowing in mind were making the boats unnecessarily tender under sail, their usual mode. He therefore redrew the Ness Boat and the Whilly Tern with this in mind, giving them a more stable shape and drawing the hulls out slightly, to create two new designs: the 16ft 10in Tirrik and the 15ft 2in Whilly Tern.

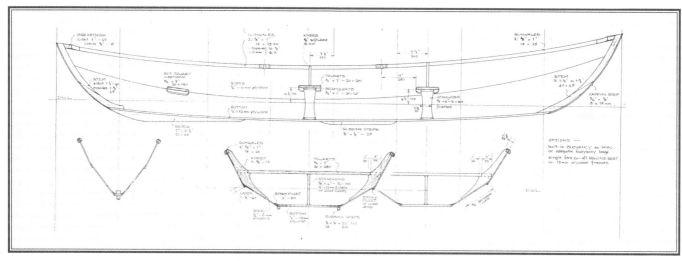

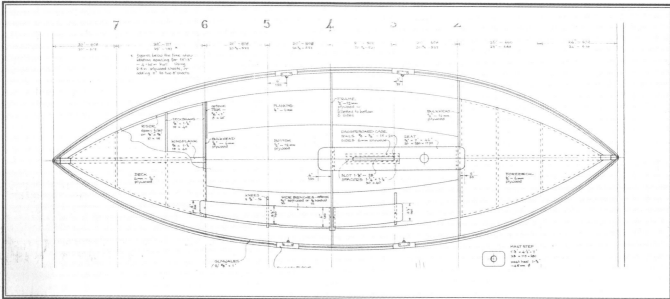

The development of Iain's double-end designs in diagrammatic form:

Skerrieskiff

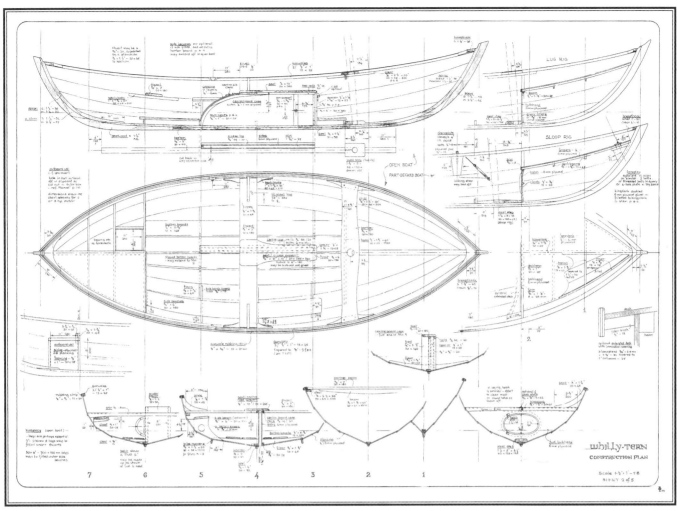

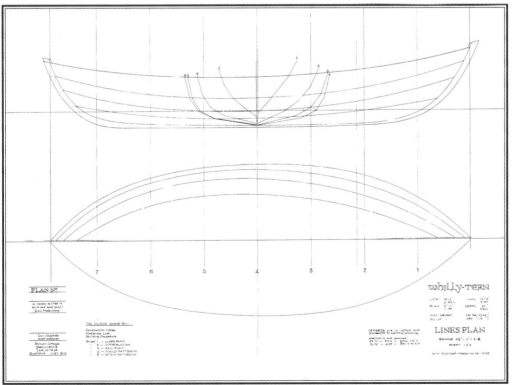

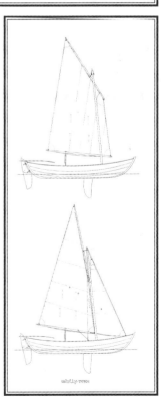

FAERINGS

It took Iain 20 years of experience as a boat designer before he felt confident enough to draw a faering, and the result is a jewel of a boat that even a Norwegian boatbuilder might feel proud of. The 15ft Elf was designed for a boatbuilding workshop run by Anton Fitzpatrick, although Iain couldn't resist subsequently building one for himself. As usual, he tested the boat in every situation to extract everything he could out of her and wrote the results up in his design notes. Although he doesn't make any great claims for her sailing abilities under sprit rig, he was very impressed by her performance under oar, particularly in rough seas. The

real clincher, however, was this:

'The supreme delight of owning this boat is in just looking at her – she is so beautiful! If I do keep her the rest of my life, I will never get weary of admiring those curves and proportions, and all their subtle interrelationships. She seems absolutely perfect from every angle! If ever a boat was a work of art . . .'

He declines to take credit for this, however, stating that all he was trying to do was create an 'authentic-looking faering'. As with many of his other designs, the Elf was stretched to 16ft 6in to become the Elfyn, which in turn was adapted for traditional construction (ie solid timber) to become the Galloway Faering (shown). The Elf also provided the basis for Iain's

100th design, the solid timber Woodfish, built by Adrian Morgan in Ullapool.

The most recent of this range is the 18ft Sula, based on the traditional 'yoals' of the Shetland Islands. Surprisingly, it is the first vessel Iain has designed from scratch for traditional construction, all his

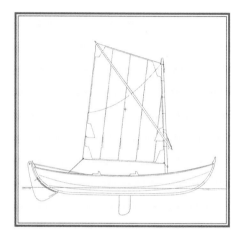

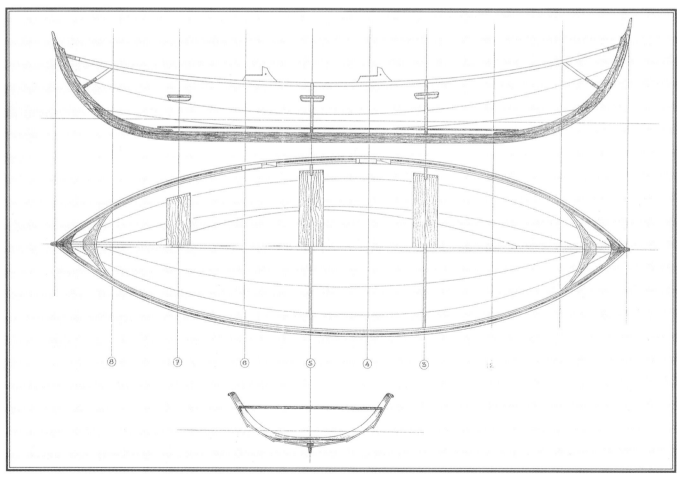

Galloway Faering

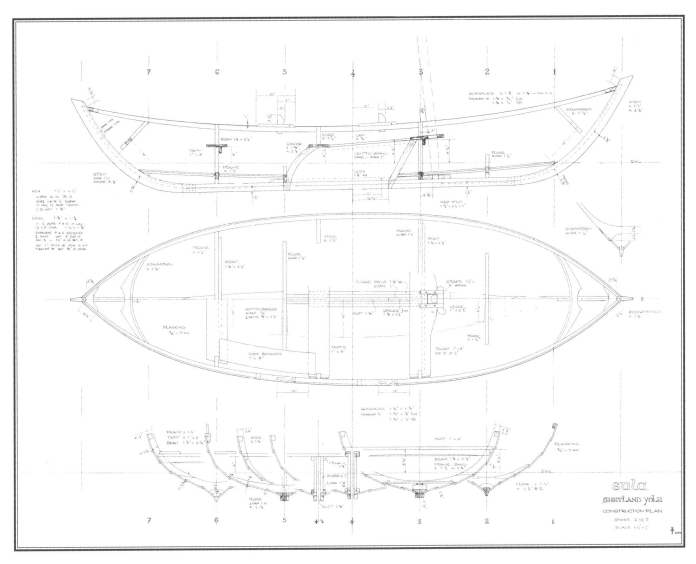

other 'traditional' boats having been designed first to be built in plywood and later adapted for solid timber. Like the faerings, Shetland yoals were originally built without the benefit of plans, and builders relied instead on rules of thumb handed down from one generation to the next. As a result, up until now there has been very little available for the amateur (or non-indigenous) builder to work from. Bearing all the hallmarks of another Oughtred classic, the Sula will hopefully change all that.

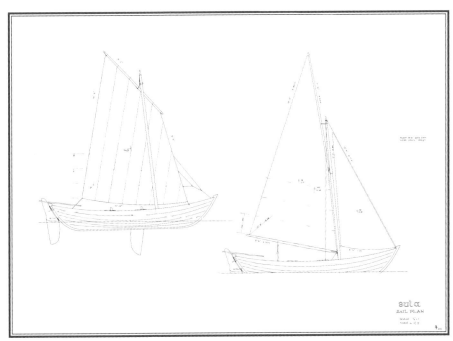

CRUISING YACHTS

Iain is better known as a designer of small boats – understandably so, considering that the majority of his designs are under 20ft long – but he has also produced a few notable gems designed for cruising. Foremost among these is the 22ft 2in Grey Seal, designed while he was on sabbatical at *WoodenBoat* in 1986, although not completed until two years later. Sometimes described as a 'small, double-ended Folkboat', its Scandinavian roots are very apparent not only in its 'pointy' stern but also its buoyant, curvaceous hull. Having drawn a centreboard version with a 2ft 3in draft, intended for transporting on a trailer and/or creek crawling, Iain

Eu na Mara

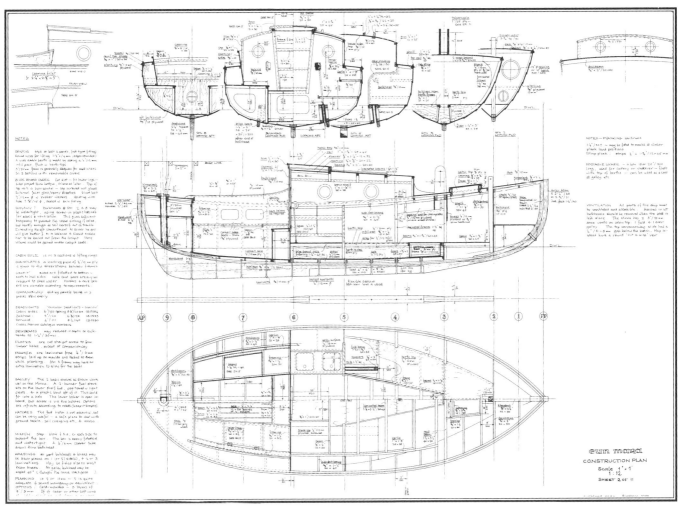

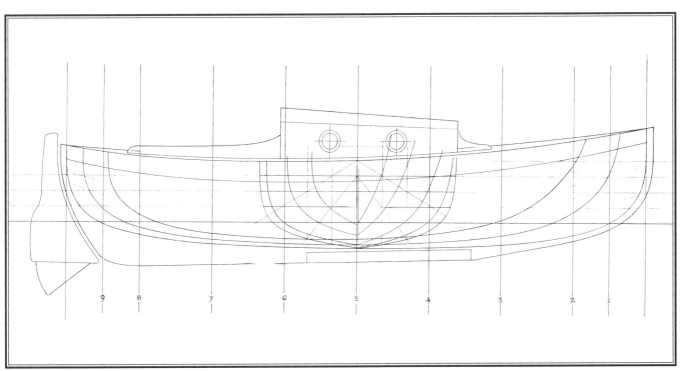

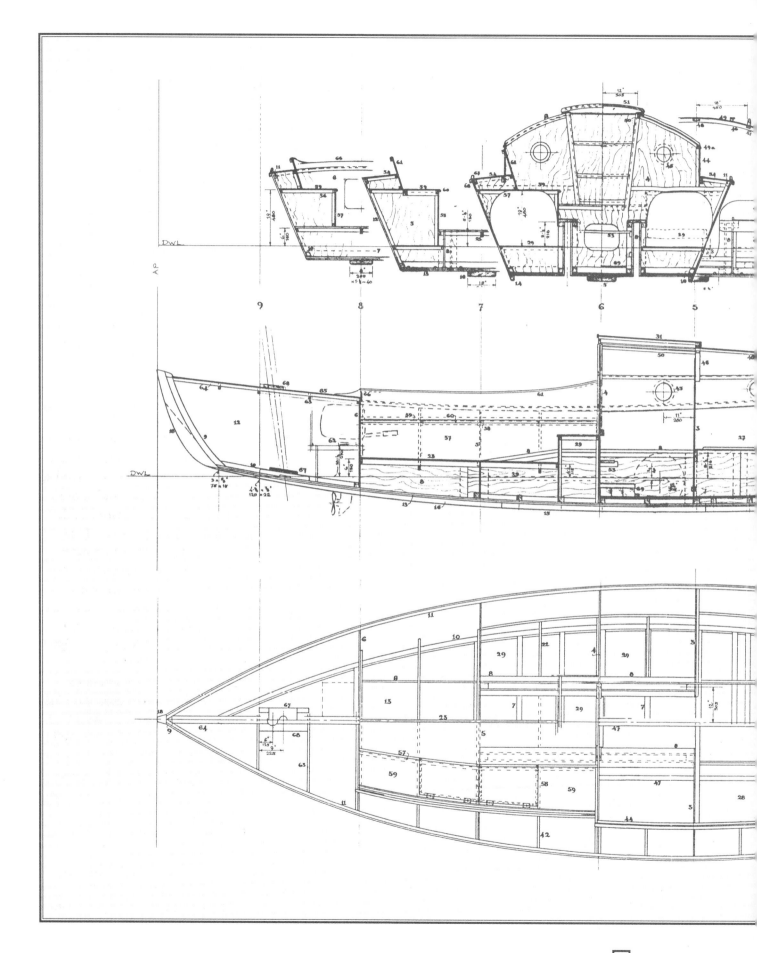

Sharpie Haiku

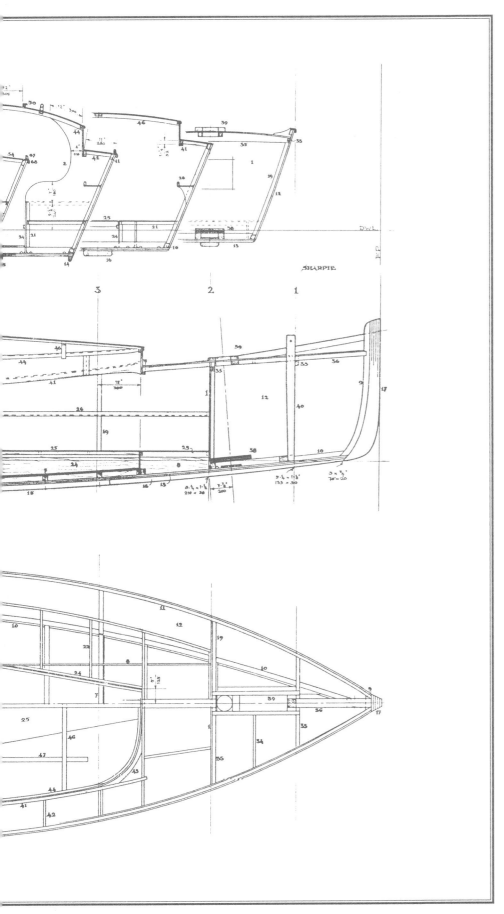

SHARPIE

3.   2.   1

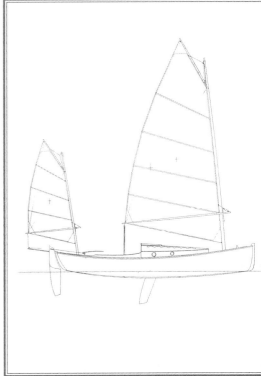

then produced a deep-keel version with 3ft 5in draft. Needless to say, other variations followed, including the 18ft 6in Wee Seal and, more recently, the 24ft 7in Super Seal.

Mike O'Brien described the genesis of the boat in an article: 'Several years ago, while Iain Oughtred was in residence here at *WoodenBoat*, discussions developed about creating plans for an able cruising boat that would be suitable for trailering and amateur construction. The transplanted Australian designer began working up some preliminary studies. As the sketches evolved, they displayed his admiration for Norwegian small craft. Well aware of the dangers involved in tampering with respected traditional types, Oughtred forged ahead, admitting simply, "I can't help it!"'

Iain has long been a fan of the canoe yawls of George Holmes and Albert Strange, so when the chance

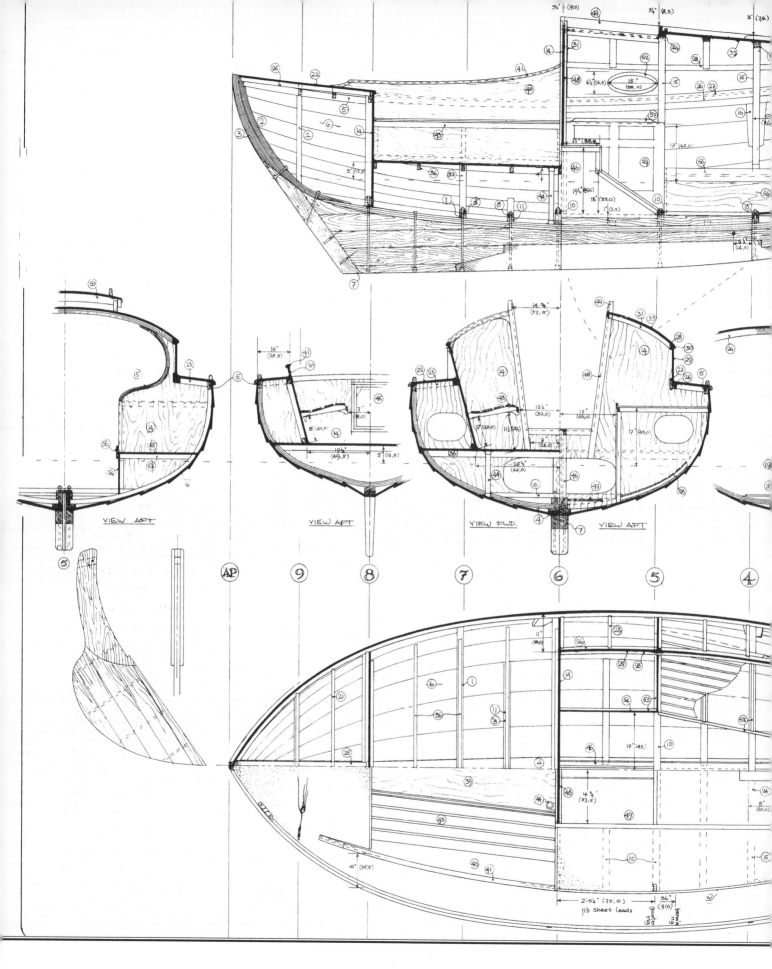

VIEW AFT

VIEW AFT

VIEW FWD.

VIEW AFT

Grey Seal

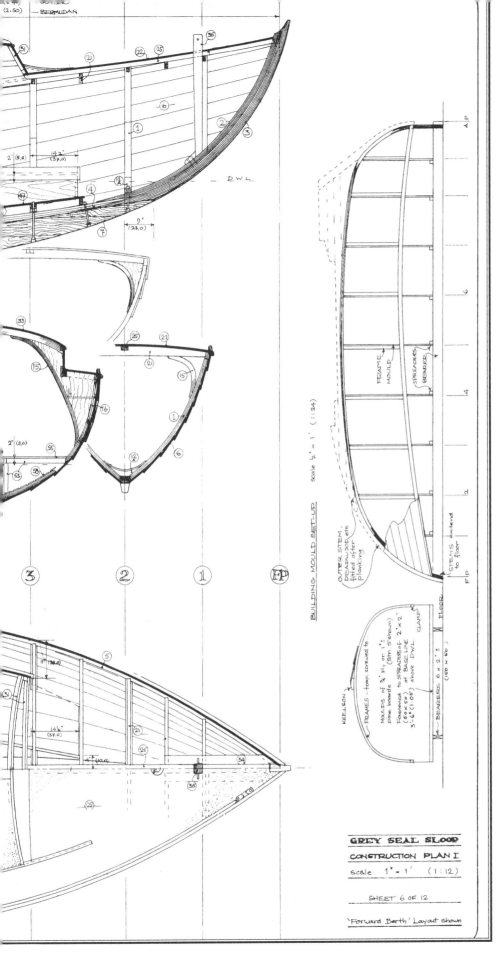

DWL

BUILDING MOULD SET-UP   Scale ½" = 1'   (1:24)

FRAME MOULD

SPREADERS

BEARDED

OUTER STEM, DEADWOOD, etc fitted after planking

STEMS extend to floor

A.P

F.P

FLOOR

KEELSON

FRAMES — temp. screwed to MOULDS of ¾" ply or 1¼" pine boards

Forward to SPREADERS of 2" × 2" (50 × 50) at BASE LINE 3' 6" (1·05) above DWL

BEARERS 6 × 2 ± (150 × 60)

CLAMP

GREY SEAL SLOOP

CONSTRUCTION PLAN I

Scale 1" = 1'   (1:12)

SHEET 6 OF 12

'Forward Berth' Layout shown

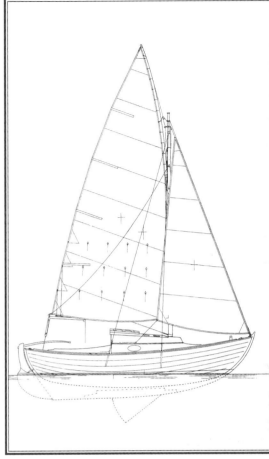

came to design a pocket cruiser to similar lines, he jumped at it. The resulting Eun Na Mara packs a lot into her 19ft 9in by 6ft 8in hull. Her beam is carried well into her ends, giving her a chubby look which gives her a distinctively 'friendly' character. There are options for a single centreboard or a pair of offcentre boards, and Iain has drawn both a gaff yawl and a gaff cutter rig – although the yawl rig seems to suit her rather better.

Iain explains the advantages of the canoe yawl shape thus: 'Canoe sterns have a way of leaving a clean wake in spite of variations of displacement, trim, and sea state. This in a sense makes the hull more adaptable than a transom-sterned boat; in a hull of limited length a designer would have a choice

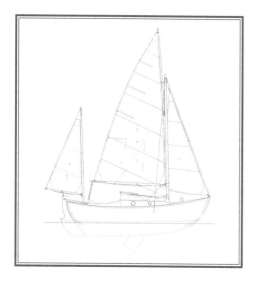

between a small transom which is more seakindly but reduces effective WL [waterline] length and buoyancy aft, or a large transom which will drag when overloaded.'

Iain's most recent new cruising design is his 30ft sharpie Haiku, which takes its inspiration from the working boats of America's East Coast. Of particular interest were the boats created by yacht designer Ralph M Munroe, who sailed his sharpie *Egret* extensively around Florida and elsewhere. Like the famous dories which evolved in the same area, the sharpies were quick and cheap to build and offered more boat for your bucks than almost any other type of craft. Iain's design is no different and, by combining a simple but effective design with modern know-how (eg hollow masts, wishbone booms), is perhaps the ultimate in minimalist sailing.

As he puts it: 'I hope that, with this combination of ancient wisdom and sensible low-tech modern developments, we will have achieved an attractive, versatile, cost-effective cruiser which will be very interesting to sail.'

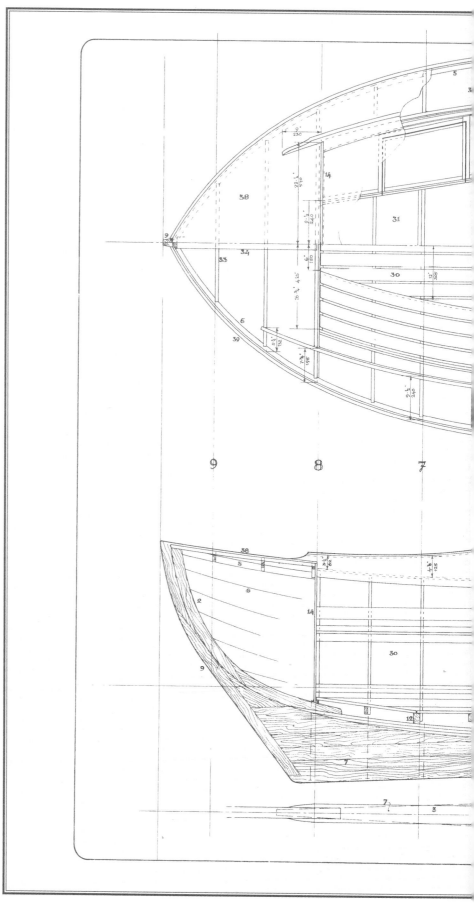

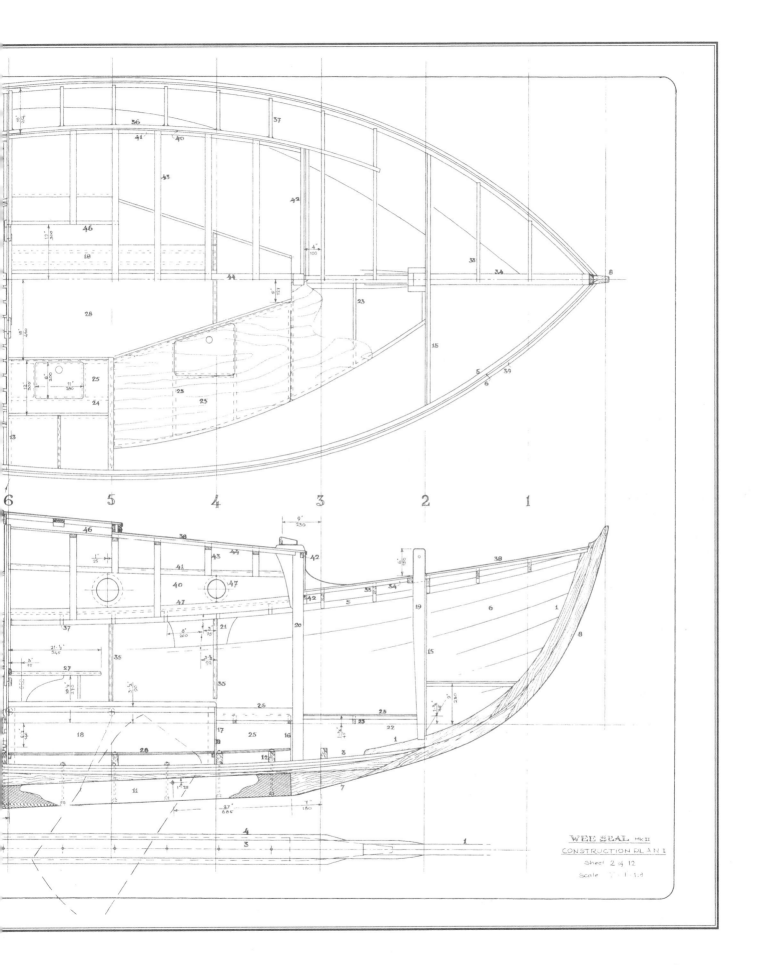

WEE SEAL MK II
CONSTRUCTION PLAN I
Sheet 2 of 12
Scale

INDEX